THE TESTIMONY OF THE SOUL

THE MACMILLAN COMPANY
NEW YORK · BOSTON · CHICAGO · DALLAS
ATLANTA · SAN FRANCISCO

MACMILLAN & CO., LIMITED
LONDON · BOMBAY · CALCUTTA
MELBOURNE

THE MACMILLAN COMPANY
OF CANADA, LIMITED
TORONTO

THE TESTIMONY
OF THE SOUL

BY

RUFUS M. JONES, LITT.D., DD., LL.D.

AUTHOR OF

*Studies in Mystical Religion, Pathways to the
Reality of God, etc.*

"The spirit of man is a candle of
the Lord." PROVERBS XX, 27

NEW YORK
THE MACMILLAN COMPANY
1936

SET UP BY BROWN BROTHERS LINOTYPERS
PRINTED IN THE UNITED STATES OF AMERICA
BY THE FERRIS PRINTING COMPANY

PREFACE

THIS volume constitutes the Ayer Lectures for 1936. The Ayer Lectureship was founded in May, 1928, in the Rochester Theological Seminary, by the gift of twenty-five thousand dollars from Mr. and Mrs. Wilfred W. Fry, of Camden, New Jersey, to perpetuate the memory of Mrs. Fry's father, the late Mr. Francis Wayland Ayer. At the time of his death Mr. Ayer was president of the corporation which maintained the Rochester Theological Seminary.

Shortly after the establishment of the Lectureship the Rochester Theological Seminary and the Colgate Theological Seminary were united under the name of the Colgate-Rochester Divinity School. It is under the auspices of this institution that the Ayer Lectures are given.

Under the terms of the Foundation the Lectures are to fall within the broad field of the history or interpretation of the Christian religion and message. It is the desire of those connected with the establishment and administration of the Lectureship that the lectures shall be religiously constructive and shall help in the building of Christian faith.

Four lectures are to be given each year at the Colgate-Rochester Divinity School at Rochester, New York, and these lectures are to be published in book form within one year after the time of their delivery. They will be known as the Ayer lectures.

The lecturer for the year 1935–36 was Professor Rufus M. Jones.

CONTENTS

Chapter I

UNEXPLORED REMAINDERS

"Battle-front" is perhaps not quite the right word to use when one is marking off the lines of the pivotal issues in religion today. I never feel happy when I hear militant terms injected into the realm of the spiritual life.

> *Onward Christian soldiers*
> *Marching as to war,*

always seems to me to fit rather badly with the spirit, the method and the way of life of the cross-bearing Leader whom the hymn intends to glorify. And yet strenuous issues confront us and the critical hour demands bravery as well as wisdom. Athanasius stood out not really "against the world" but against a widespread form of Christianity which seemed to him to be "heretical." The alternative to his type of Christianity was another interpretation of Christianity which seemed to him of a distinctly lower grade. But even so the issue in which he was the champion was not Christianity *or* no religion at all.

That situation, or a similar one, has been true in

most of the "battle-epochs" of history. "Orthodoxy" has been pitted against what it chose to call "heterodoxy," but in most instances the latter was as fervently, as intensely, *religious* as was the former. The alternative was always religion in another form. Today the pivotal issue has profoundly shifted. The religious attitude itself is challenged. The religious view of life as such is questioned. The validity of a spiritual outlook of any kind is put in jeopardy. The alternative to religious faith today is the acceptance of a naturalistic universe, a biologized man, a secularized society. Meantime the issues between the conservatives and the liberals, between the fundamentalists and the modernists, between the high church and the broad church wings seem like petty controversies, when the whole house in which the contestants are living is on fire and in deadly peril.

For a vast section of the human race religion today is declared to be "an opiate." It is thought of as a cunningly devised method of making the masses submissive to their overlords or their over-shepherds, and of lulling them into a dull acceptance of the hard present conditions of life by an imaginary vision of relief which is to be realized in a world to come. Religion is discounted as a scheme of drugging the victim with imaginary hopes and fears instead of with opium or with vodka.

This conception of religion as "opiate" is by no

means confined to Russia. It has been caught up as a comfortable slogan by hosts of youth who are in a state of revolt from the inadequate interpretations of Christianity in their homes and in their childhood churches and Sunday schools. They have done almost no *thinking* about the deeper issues of life. They have blindly revolted against an inherited system that has lost its attraction, and they have caught up a popular "rationalization," which gives them a temporary relief from what seem to them the "burdens" of religion. Parents in their agony and ministers in their perplexity find themselves helpless. They are confronted by a "drift" like that which carries the sand of the desert over the vegetation of border countries. It is not a position which has been arrived at by intelligent processes of thought and which can consequently be answered by the reasoning mind. It is a confused "drift" of blind forces, urges, moods, inchoate attitudes, rather than a set of reasoned ideas which can be met in a stand-up, give and take, debate.

Then, again, we find ourselves today confronted with the central issue of what "civilization" is to mean in this post-war world. Have we perhaps left forever behind the comfortable world in which the free individual can be captain of his own soul, can think his own thoughts, plan his own career, and shape his own destiny as a person? Or is man—and woman too—to be a mechanized unit in a totalitarian state, to be regimented from outside, ruled as the wheel rules the spoke, and used as *a means,* as a passive instrument, for the ends of a completely secularized state? In a "civilization" of that latter type there can be no place for free, spontaneous, creative religion as a joyous response of the individual person to a higher invisible order of values and realities, for the totalitarian state is conceived already to be the highest reality and value, to which every knee must bow and every arm salute. This "civilization" is not a return to "paganism." It is not a "restoration" of the gods Odin and Thor. They— with paganism—belong to a past which is forever "dead." That primitive period of life was intensely, throbbingly, religious. It was alive with *faith* and *vision.* It was a crude faith, no doubt, and the vision was distorted, but it was nevertheless man's sincere attempt to adjust his life to invisible and eternal realities, greater than himself. That simple stage of life cannot be "restored." That early faith and that childlike vision do not fit the world-outlook of today.

The alternative tendency that is being adopted is, not to find the way down to a deeper faith, or to widen the vision to fit the whole field of reality, but to accept instead a social-economic theory of life as a substitute for religion, and to put the temporal state in the place of the eternal Fatherland of the soul. It is, again, not alone in one country that this severe "reduction" of life is under way. The "drift" toward a secularized world in one form or another is widespread, and it is an ominous mood. "Earth is enough" is one of its articles of confession. "The comfortable conjugation of the verb to eat" is accepted as "the supreme end of man." It is not enough. It will not do. We men cannot *live* that way. There is a "remainder"—a precious remnant of life—which needs to be explored. There are *implications* which our kind of life forces upon us. They need to be seriously dealt with. There is an interior *depth-life* in man that carries rich veins of wealth which should be carefully assayed. The historical trails to the headwaters of our faith are being profoundly searched today and these historical researches are accumulating stores of spiritual riches. We need not tremble for the preservation of the truth which History enshrines. It will not be lost.

I am more concerned for the exploration of the light and truth which attach inherently to the fundamental nature of man's spiritual central self. I want its testimony. In his address to the primitive-minded people of Lycaonia, St. Paul said: "God has not left Himself without witness" (Acts *XIV*, 17). It is a great saying. The soul itself is a witness. It has its own testimony to bear—a testimony of a higher range and order than that of mountains and nebulae, or the rising and setting of autumnal stars. Tertullian was not always in the order of "the prophets of the soul." But in his *De testimonio animae* there is a noble passage which sounds as modern as though it were written yesterday. I give it greatly reduced and fore-shortened, but even so it has the ring of reality: "I call in a new testimony. . . . Stand forth O soul . . . from whatever source, and in whatever way, thou makest man a rational being, in the highest degree capable of thought and knowledge—stand forth and give thy witness. I call thee not as, when fashioned in schools, trained in libraries, fed up in Attic academies and porticoes, thou belchest forth wisdom. I address thee, simple and rude, uncultured and untaught, such as they have thee who have thee only; that very thing pure and entire, of the road, the street, the workshop. *I want thy experience.* I demand of thee the things thou bringest with thee into man, which thou knowest either from thyself, or from thy author, whoever he may be." Then with a flash of prophet's insight he draws his conclusion: "Whenever the soul comes to itself, as out of a surfeit, or a sleep, or a sickness, and attains something of its natural soundness, *it speaks of God. There is not a soul of man that does not, from the light that is in itself, proclaim God."* (Italics mine.)

I want to come back to that "precious remainder" in our lives which is so apt to be overlooked or forgotten and which needs to be explored. When the five thousand were fed by the northern shore of Gennesaret, one of the marvels of the feeding was the overplus remainder of twelve baskets of food gathered up from unused fragments. There is no mention made of the further disposal of this surprising remainder. The account stops abruptly there. The rest is silence. It is apt to be so with remainders. They are usually left unexplored. We have never heard, we never shall hear, what became of the unused spices which were brought by the women to the sepulchre on the morning of the resurrection. There is no hint of the disposal of these precious gifts which love had prepared.

Every great epic of the race presents merely a *selection* out of the events which glorified the dim magnificence of the cradle period of history which the particular epic celebrates and only a very few of the heroes of any people ever get crowned or haloed in the annals which survive. Homer did not create his heroes. He found them living in the memory of his contemporaries, and he passed over in silence the vast unexplored remainder who failed to get their deeds preserved in the amber of men's memory. Not half of any block of marble is preserved when it serves a sculptor as the substance for the expression of his vision. Day after day he cuts off marble chips which pile up under his work and are carried off to fill rubbish heaps. We never hear again of these chips. They are a part of the world's "waste." They have no further interest for us any more than has the chaff after the wheat is pounded out. It is said, probably as a legend, that Michelangelo *saw* his "Moses" in the unhewn block of marble, but what the spectators saw who watched him carve it

was vast heaps of marble chips flying off under the
strokes of his mallet. The "waste" of marble was
much more in evidence than was the artist's conception
of the great law-giver. And yet only the figure which
the artist saw in his mind has become immortal. The
rest has vanished unnoted. The more than twelve
basketsful of débris from the sculptor's shop remain
unexplored. In this case the fragments seem unimportant; the priceless treasure is the immortal figure of
Moses.

It is so, again, with the mass of pitchblende which
produces the precious grain of radium. Madame Curie
discovered that in some mysterious way the piece of
pitchblende, which her Polish friends out of curiosity
sent to her, altered the photographic plates which were
in the safe where she put the pitchblende. She there-
upon began a searching analysis of the mysterious rock.
She dissolved away with her chemicals what seemed to
be the main substance of the pitchblende and behold,
she discovered a tiny nucleus of remainder which
proved to be the new element that has revolutionized
all our conceptions of matter and opened up a long
train of further discoveries.

How little of the life of any one of us ever gets expressed. When André Chenier, the young French poet,
climbed the stairs to the guillotine in the Reign of
Terror he said, "It's too bad to cut off that head of
mine. There's something inside it!" We all feel that

way about our heads, I think, even when they are not being cut off by the guillotine. There is something inside that we never quite get out. We are something more than our best friends ever know. The world makes up its mind about us and tickets us off, but life within ourselves has a secret meaning which will never get known or expressed. We shall carry to our graves an unexplored remainder—we are doomed to be "unknown men."

The most striking of all our unexplored remainders is what is left out and ignored in the abstractive process of analysis which is characteristic of the scientific method. In its passion for clarity, for exactness of description, and for completely impersonal explanation, science has been compelled to *reduce* the phenomena with which it can deal adequately and to seize just those aspects of the world which will submit to exact description and explanation. It is often true that the scientist is himself unconscious of the *reduction* which he is making. He thinks that he is dealing with all that is *there* in the field which he is studying, but there are always impalpables and imponderables that slip through his net and escape him.

The mathematical aspects, the general universal aspects, the space-time, or physical-mechanical, aspects are the ones, of course, which most naturally and easily fit the scientific methods of description and explanation. Just these aspects have consequently been in the

foreground and centre of scientific procedure ever since
Newton's day. They are easily caught in his net. But
obviously the abstractive method which the scientist is
bound to use cannot be applied to our rich and crowded
universe without leaving out of account an immensely
important remainder of imponderables. So long as we
are dealing with the lines and figures of pure mathematics the reductions which the scientist makes are negligible. The lines we draw and the figures we make with
chalk or pencil are always wavy and never perfectly
straight. Furthermore all the lines we draw have width.
The abstractive lines and figures of pure mathematics are
freed from these well-known qualities of width and
variation. Something has gone from our real world
of experience when we reduce our figures to pure
forms, but we do not miss the remainder or feel its
loss.

Our exact accounts of even the simplest and "mean-
est" things in nature, in like manner, *reduce* them to a
greater simplicity and nakedness than really exist in
fact. We deal with them in their universal aspect, not
in their concrete particular variations. The botanist's
leaf or flower is denuded of its own peculiar features
and it blurs off into a common species which can be
once for all described. The poet's flower is very different from that of the botanist and carries a precious
remainder which the botanist has lost. It is even more
so, of course, with the higher forms of life. An incal-

culable element appears wherever life unfolds. There is a factor of spontaneity, however slight, wherever there is life, and the processes of it are never quite absolutely predictable. But we know well enough what an amoeba will do under given circumstances. And we are confident that we can lay down once for all the biographical facts of the black beetle. Even so no general biological account of the species does quite do full and absolute justice to "the inner life" of a particular black beetle in the heyday of his own unique existence! He would not recognize as adequate even the best scientific account of himself.

The "remainder," however, in this case is so slight, so unimportant, that we cannot stop to bother with it. We quite rightly ignore it as negligible. It is another matter when we pass higher up and begin to deal with human emotions, or with values of life, or especially with personality itself. Here the overplus, the remainder, which floods over the scientific description, has a rare quintessence of richness and worth. The most perfect psychological account of love leaves the reader of it very cold and very far away from the concrete reality. The throb and thrill are somehow left out. It is an empty shell with the life gone out of it. It is no less so with all those traits of life which we experience as our supreme intrinsic values. We find ourselves strangely inarticulate when we endeavor to express our joy over a beautiful creation or when we undertake to define our moral passion for what ought to be or when we burst through all barriers and discover a truth which defies all attempts to doubt it.

When the scientist tries to *reduce* these high experiences of the soul to a naturalistic basis and laboriously endeavors to "explain" them in terms of inheritance from lower forms, or as aids to survival, or as environmental influences, or as accidental variations, there is just where "the unexplored remainder" completely overtops in importance the exact account which has been presented. There are at least twelve basketsful of leftovers. We are caught here in *the genetic fallacy*. The genetic method is the attempt to explain things in terms of their origins and earlier stages rather than in terms of their fully developed state. It is assumed that the simpler and more perfectly definable forms are nearer the exact nature of reality than are the higher and more complex ones. But in actual fact we never find out what a fully developed reality is by discovering what it was when it *began to be*. If what we were dealing with were wholly quantitative, and were the mere addition of facts, we might get on by going back to the simple unit, but the genetic method fails to work completely when we are dealing with things which take on new and strikingly other *qualities* of reality in the process of development. The genetic method leaves out vast basketsful of remainder. Aristotle was much nearer the truth when he said:

"The true nature of a thing is the highest that it can become."

When it comes to a question of what we may call the *Heart of the whole matter* the "reduction" then becomes so much the more obvious and so much the more tragic. The central life within the person, and the central World of spiritual reality within the visible world which we describe, are bound to elude our most exact methods of reporting and explaining. There is something all the time presupposed which nevertheless cannot be spread out and dealt with as an object for us. The eye which beholds cannot look at itself. The camera which catches all objects in its field always fails to photograph itself. Somewhat so that which is highest and truest and most real and most precious for our deepest life cannot come before the footlights of the observing mind of the beholder. It gets omitted in the description. It is the supreme "unexplored remainder." When we omit the testimony of the soul, we no longer talk of twelve basketsful of overplus, for the remainder which overtops our explorations turns out to be the most important part of the whole world and that for which all the rest exists.

CHAPTER II

RECOVERY OF THE LOST RADIANCE

L. P. JACKS some years ago wrote a remarkable essay on "The Lost Radiance of Christianity." I am sorry to say that with too many Christians that radiance and joy which characterized the first Christians is still lost. We have insisted upon orthodoxy as the test of faith and it has hardly entered into the heart of man to conceive how much more important it is to discover how to live in the midst of the difficulties of this complicated world, and in the round of toil, with joy and radiance and power. Too many of us are so busy thinking and speculating and arguing that we find little time to restore our souls, as the beloved Psalmist knew how to do, and to get the deep-lying springs of life set free within us.

The most effective Christian method is not that of argument and debate as the forums suppose. The greatest things in the world are not reached by arguing. You can never argue anybody into loving you! The great experiences of life come like a vernal equinox or like a luminous beam of light, and then there is no longer any need of arguing, you find yourself securely in the presence of an immutable fact of life. What I miss most in our present-day Christianity with its confusions and

controversies is the spirit of serenity, of gentleness, of
simplicity, of tenderness and grace, that love which
suffers long and is kind, that depth and power of sacrifice which were so marvelous in the life of Jesus. An
ounce of that spirit weighs more than a ton of abstract
doctrine.

We need to find our way back to the central sources
of life and inspiration. We must learn how to deal
with the issues of life in our time as profoundly and
as seriously as the fourth-century Christians dealt with
the abstract problems of creed and doctrine, and with
that constructive power of genius which the builders of
the Gothic cathedrals showed in the twelfth and thirteenth centuries. If religion cannot be made a way of
life it becomes a negligible luxury which we may as
well drop from our minds, and devote ourselves to conjugating the verb "to eat." The moment Christianity
becomes thoroughly alive it always has a way of doing
miraculous things. It changes water to wine, it brings
prodigals home, it raises life out of death, it turns
sunsets to sunrises, it makes the lame man walk and
the blind man see.

If we are to bring religion back into vital dominion
over men's lives in the world today and make it live
again as a creative power it will not be done by our
clever arguments. There is a counter-argument for
every argument any one of us has in his quiver. The
only glowing refutation of the materialism and secular-

ism of our time is a personal life which demonstrates a source of spiritual power. We must therefore become experts in the cultivation of the spiritual fruits of life rather than clever theorists and speculators. We have hardly begun to reach the full significance of Christianity as a way of life because we have been busy with the periphery of it instead of with the center of it. We have too often thought of it as a theory instead of a joyous experience.

The old infallibilities are dead and they must be replaced, not by new infallibilities, but by fresh discoveries of God and by the living testimony of the awakened soul. Plato always insisted that man's soul is attached to God by its root. In fact there is no other possible origin of a spiritually endowed soul except God who is Spirit. The great mystics have always known that to be so and they have based their religious hopes and expectations on that sure foundation. It may be taken as a primary truth that God has already *found us* long before we are consciously seeking Him. George Macdonald's poem of the little child's experience beautifully expresses this primary truth and describes what at some high moment we all feel when we "become as little children."

> *I am a little child and I*
> *   Am ignorant and weak;*
> *I gaze into the starry sky*
> *   And then I cannot speak;*

For all behind the starry sky,
  Behind the world so broad,
Behind men's hearts and souls doth lie
  The infinite of God.

There are ways of seeing and knowing as by a lightning flash of intuitive insight which brings us much closer to the heart of reality than our sterile thinking by abstract concepts ever can do.

We should lose our conviction of the reality of the external world if we lost all sense contacts with it. If to use Hamlet's word we had no "speculation" in our eyes and saw nothing when we looked outward; if our ears heard nothing when we listened; if our fingers found nothing when we "palpitated" with them; if our muscular and joint senses found no resistance anywhere in space to push against, our world out there would fade away and vanish into dream or myth. It is very much so, I think, with the reality of God. We cannot hold on to it and keep it vivid and vital if our conviction of it rests solely on the testimony of ancient books and doctrines, or on mere logical inferences.

Imagine what would happen to us if no one of us had ever seen a sunrise or a sunset and all our knowledge of rising and setting suns rested entirely on what we could learn by research in Assyrian clay tablets or Egyptian papyri, written by men who had seen these events three thousand years ago. If we expect religion to be the supreme dynamic of our lives—and if it isn't *that,* what is it?—then God must possess us with a faith that is born of first-hand conviction. We must stop being disciples of Lot's wife who lost her chance of life by a persistent backward gaze when all the hope there was lay in front of her. The day-dawn and the day-star must rise in our own hearts.

That faith is hardly likely to be born in us unless we have a central philosophy which gives us ground for believing that there is a sphere of spiritual reality—a divine taproot—in the very foundation of man's being and that the ultimate nature of the universe is more like the spirit in ourselves than it is like anything else in the world. I have so often interpreted that philosophical position—and shall do so again in later chapters—that I leave it now and proceed to speak simply of those facts of experience which seem to me to verify the claims of that philosophy.

There are occasions in life, and they are assuredly our highest moments, when the individual soul obtains its own vision, sees for itself, and is aware of "a divine mutual and reciprocal correspondence" with this environment of the Spirit, in which we live and move and are. We are amphibious beings, as Plotinus used to say. We are able to correspond with an environment of space and time, in which we learn how successfully to conjugate the verb "to eat," *and* at the same time we are also so made that we can, and in fact must, correspond with *the real world* which fits our inmost needs.

There is a remarkable instance of living in these two worlds, given in the *Book of Revelation*. The writer of it says in his prelude that he was "in Patmos" and that he was "in the Spirit." He was a prisoner on that volcanic island, a toiler in the mines in which the prisoners worked. He was in a hard and stubborn temporal and spatial environment. He did not find his relief and restoration by evasion, by refusing to accept the world of his toil and struggle. He found his *real world* just there where he was—"I was in Patmos and in the Spirit."

The deeper real environment anticipates our need of it. It *operates* vitally upon us. We feel a pull toward that dear Fatherland of the Spirit to which we "belong." We are "restless" until we are "at home" in the true realm of life for which we are made, until we say: "I will arise and go to my Father." When we see the robe in place of the rags, the shoes on the feet weary of travel in a far country, the ring of love on the finger, and feel the kiss of recognition on the cheek, there comes a transfigured conviction that we "belong."

It is not a peaceful heaven beyond the stars that we are seeking. It is not some place "yonder" that concerns us. It is the here and now. The discourse is about another level of life here in the midst of time. There are moments when we are aware of the real world, the home of the soul, the goal of the pilgrimage. We find ourselves in "mutual and reciprocal correspondence" with that real world. There comes a palpitating sense that the Above and the below have come together. The glow in the iron means that the fire has penetrated it. The sensitiveness of the needle to the magnetic currents, in which it moves, reveals the fact that it itself has been magnetized and transformed. This heightened sense of correspondence which comes in high moments, this feeling of parallelism with divine currents, means that the central stream of Life has broken in and penetrated the soul with energies beyond itself.

When this happens a person feels refreshed as though by God's own breath. He passes from argument to quiet assurance and from the dusty road of words and talk to certainties of life. "If thou wouldst be perfect," Meister Eckhart said, "thou wilt not *prate* about God." It is as though Eternity broke into time, and life overbrimmed with the joy and fortification of incoming tides of energy.

My beloved teacher, Josiah Royce, used to tell us of a conviction of faith which "enables a man to stand anything that can happen to him in the universe." Alice James, William James' sister, lifelong invalid and baffled soul, had an experience of which she wrote: "My mind was suddenly flooded by one of those luminous waves that sweep out of consciousness all but the living sense, and overpower one with joy in the rich throbbing complexity of life." And George Fox, in the

power of his transforming experience—an experience
which gave the whole creation a new smell—said: "I
saw that there was an ocean of darkness and death, but
I *saw* that there was an infinite Ocean of light and love
which flowed over the ocean of darkness." Pascal, in
the mighty sweep of currents which invaded him, could
only ejaculate the words: "Certainty, joy, certainty,
feeling, sight, joy. Joy, Joy, tears of Joy." Like the
fragrance of Mary's ointment which pervaded the
house of Bethany, this installment of life remained for
the rest of Pascal's days a penetrating power of grace
and strength.

This overbrimming experience of "fresh initiation
into life" is perhaps a rare occurrence. The highest
ranges of human achievement presuppose a person of
peculiar gifts and aptitudes. Very few of us leap to
the full height of appreciation of great music. And not
many of us can *love* as the Brownings did.

But I maintain that mutual fellowship with God
is as truly a normal trait of human life as breathing
is. If, as I believe, the soul has its root in God, it
should not be strange or amazing that fresh install-
ments of life break in from beyond us and refresh
us. There is a type of *organic mysticism* which is
much more common than highly conscious mysticism
is. There are persons all about us who *practice* the
presence of God without having had a definite experience of invasion which they could date or report. They

walk among us with radiance and joy, but they wist not
that their faces shine.

> As torrents in summer,
> Half dried in their channels,
> Suddenly rise, though the
> Sky is still cloudless,
> For rain has been falling
> Far off at their fountains;
>
> So hearts that are fainting
> Grow full to o'erflowing;
> And they that behold it
> Marvel and know not
> That God at their fountains
> Far off hath been raining.[1]

Times of hush and meditation, "recollection" and
integration, bring resources to live by as well as health
and restoration. Serenity comes not alone by removing
the outward causes and occasions of fear, but by the
discovery of inward reservoirs of strength to draw
upon. There are deeps in us below the level of our own
thoughts and ideas. There is a substratum in us that is
the mother soil of all our thinking and of all our
doing, out of which our ideas and ideals emerge, "as
capes of cloud out of the invisible air." To feed, or to
fertilize, this subsoil of our lives is vastly more important than to pick up and exploit a few more random ideas. In fact, that former attainment is the

[1] Longfellow: *Tales of a Wayside Inn.*

master secret of life. Increase in depth and power of life is in every way more important than knowing so many things, most of which may not be so. The great mystics speak much of "interior plenitude," "amplitude of life," "spiritual fecundity," and we may take it as settled that inward resources are the best assets that life has to show.

The supreme evidence that something real and transforming has happened through such an experience is the increased integration of the person's life. What counts most is moral fortification, sensitivity of spirit, quickened spiritual vitality, increased tenderness, and heightened power to stand "the heavy and weary weight" of daily toil and grind. It is not ecstasy that matters. Ecstasy carries no convincing evidence of the soul's arrival at reality. There is nothing sacred, nothing spiritual, in ecstasy, any more than there is in hypnosis. There are many ways of inducing states which are characterized by intensified *oneness*, absence of *otherness*, with suspension of critical attitudes, but these states, as such, have no special spiritual value, though they may well become preparatory occasions for higher processes of life to break through. Bergson very well says that "the great mystic does not stop at ecstasy as at the end of a journey. The ecstasy is indeed rest, but as though at a station where the engine is still under steam, until it is time to race forward again." [2]

[2] Bergson, H., *Morality and Religion*, p. 219.

Mere emotional uplift is again no more valuable as evidence or as asset than ecstasy is. Emotions are often like mirages. They may suggest reality when there is nothing real in the offing to gush about. But on the other hand there are emotions of a higher order which rise out of the deeps of experience, are the overtones of real discovery and become the driving forces toward great action. The important test, then, is neither ecstasy nor emotion. It is rather integration of personality, moral fortification of life, and preparation for creative living.

The ultimate effect of contact with the central stream of life is a vast increase of both the joy and the power of life. There comes a sense of fusion of the finite and the infinite, a unification of the surface consciousness with the deeps which underlie it and with it an *élan vital* which dynamizes the life of action. The sense of "belonging"—"He is mine and I am His"—makes life feel like a new creation, and the assurance that "God is for us" helps to eliminate the paralysis of fear as well as of pessimism, or of cynicism. There comes a fine union of serenity and adventure.

Two questions remain: (1) How does mystical experience affect one's social tasks, and (2) Is there any technique which prepares for mystical experience? Abbé Huvelin said once, "If a man should say to me, 'Today I saw God,' I should ask him, 'How do you feel now that you know God is so near you?' " I should go a step beyond that and ask, How does this experience of yours affect the main business of life? What difference does it make in your impact on the world?

It has often been assumed by the critics of mysticism that the experiences which I have been describing act as a kind of opiate, or intoxication, and carry the person who is a recipient into a comfortable quietism. "God's in His heaven; all's right with the world!" It is supposed that mystical experience is an end in itself. The person finds God, or thinks he does, and *that* is his *terminus ad quem*. He strains after this exalted experience and when he gets it, he lets the old world "stew in its own juice," while he becomes a "Pollyanna," and enjoys his retreat in "Beulah land."

Just the opposite of that is the normal effect of genuine mystical experience. The great mystics come back from their high moments with an imperative sense of mission in the world. Almost no major mystics have ever approved of quietism. The Seraphim of Isaiah's vision are a perfect symbol of the right attitude of one who has *seen*. Each one had six wings. With two of these powers of activity he covered his face as a mark of awe and reverence; with two of them he covered himself out of sight in complete humility, "and with twain he did fly" in joyous service. Reverence, humility and action are expressed by the symbol of the wings of the Seraphim, the highest order in the angelic series.

And the prophet himself terminated his vision with the significant words: "Here am I, send me."

Meister Eckhart in the fourteenth century used to rank Martha above Mary, but either Martha, the figure of activity, or Mary, the figure of contemplation, alone is a futile half of a life—a divided self. The fuss and drive and worry of Martha spoil her activity as she rushes about to prepare a splurge meal for a guest, while the absorption of Mary in a rapture when there was work which needed her, makes her piety thin and ineffective.

Phillips Brooks used to tell of a missionary who came home on furlough from his field in Africa. On his return to Africa he took out to his people a sundial which he thought would be of great practical value to the community. The simple-minded people were, however, so filled with wonder and admiration over the marvelous mechanism that they immediately built a roof over it to guard it carefully from rain and sun! There are no doubt types of religious piety much like that, and there have been individual mystics who have endeavored to insulate their high experiences from contact with the world where action lies. Plotinus in a mistaken moment said, "Action is a weakening of contemplation." The experience of contemplation for him must be a thing apart. It must be hedged about and segregated from the turmoil of life. "Let us build three tabernacles," say the disciples on the Mount of Transfiguration, "and remain and gaze." "Let us put a roof

over our rare and unique vision of God." But I maintain that mysticism at its best and truest has usually
been a way of intensified *life,* a girding of the soul for
action.

We are only too familiar with an opposite type of
religious activity which is busy and nervous and "crea-
turely," but without the depth and serenity which come
from contact with the central Source of Life. The Old
Testament character, Ahimaaz, admirably illustrates the
type. He was a famous runner—a pre-Marathon sprin-
ter—in the days of David and his captain Joab. Joab
had won a great victory and wished to send a fleet
messenger to inform the king. But it was essential that
the messenger should have been present at the affair,
should have seen with his own eyes what had happened, and could transmit the details of the event. Joab
called for volunteers for the service. Up came Ahimaaz, panting to be on the go. "Let me run," he said.
"But wherefore wouldst thou run," said Joab, "seeing
that thou hast no tidings, not having been there?"
"Nevertheless," this typical activist replied, "let me
run." There are Ahimaazes today in almost every
church and on most committees. They are of both
sexes. They have not "been there." They have no
authentic tidings, but they are fine examples of speed
and they are famous for "doing things." /

What I am concerned about is to get these two types
—the Mary and Martha types—these two halves of
life, fused into a unified person. Or better still, as

James Martineau pointed out in his great sermon on *The Tides of the Spirit,* religious life should be rhythmical, with moments of refreshment and restoration in the life of God, alternating with constructive tasks in the busy world of affairs. Mystical intuition ought to make hundred candle-power, and hundred horse-power, persons, and it often does make them. The conviction and depth, the poise and serenity, which come through contact with God, make a tremendously effective organ of creative work.

But mystical experience does not supply a ready-made plan or pattern of what is to be done in the world. It brings a vital urge, an *élan vital,* to life, but not a miraculous solution of life's problems, or a vision of relief for all human ills. Detailed *guidance* is not quite so easy, nor so simple a matter as ancient Quakers believed, or as modern Oxford groupers suppose. Consciousness of spiritual direction is a slow deposit of life and experience, like insight in poetry and music, or like taste in art. It is a slowly ripened fruit which grows on the tree of life, somewhat as moral dexterity of conduct does, or much as the technique of a gentleman is acquired. We had better not look for miraculous interventions to achieve those ends of life which have been put within the sphere of our own spiritualized capacities, coöperating with God. I am cautious about expecting secret messages from sociable angels.

We come finally to the question of *technique.* I am convinced that the mystical way will always remain a way of surprise and wonder rather than a beaten and regimented road of travel with a Baedeker guide-book. It is a path which "the falcon's eye hath not seen," nor has any traveler charted the trail for all other voyagers. When we succeed in mapping the way of producing music like that of Bach or Beethoven, or how to write poetry like *Tintern Abbey,* perhaps we can tell what ladders of the spirit will carry us up to a meeting place with God.

The technique of Yoga, or of the Zen Buddhists, is a discipline of very high order for the control of sense, of muscles, of imagination, of wandering thoughts, of human passions, but in neither case does it guarantee that at the end of its long hard road there will be the desired meeting place—the Bethel of the soul. Routine, cut-and-dried systems of discipline may help to make a Stoic temper or to prepare a climber of Mount Everest, or to forge a mystic of the type of St. John of the Cross, but these disciplines seem to me to be too doctrinaire and too remote from life to be satisfactory ways into the heart of divine reality.

I am interested in a mysticism which brings life to its full, rich goal of complete living, with radiance and joy and creative power. Preparation through appreciation of *beauty,* learning how to sound the deeps of *love,* formation of purity, gentleness, tenderness of heart, freedom from harshness of judgment, absolute honesty of purpose and motive—these positive traits and qualities of life are far more important steps on the inner pathway than are artificial techniques of discipline.

What counts most is the fellowship and influence of spiritually contagious persons who, beholding as in a mirror the glory of the Lord, unconsciously transmit that Life. Great literature, written by persons who have been there and who have the gift of vividly interpreting their inner life, is one of the most vital influences toward the discovery of the way. "Does not our heart burn as we go in the way" with the luminous souls who have found the path ahead of us and who can tell us how it fared with them?

Expectation, which is another name for faith, is essential for any high achievement, and of course is peculiarly important in this supreme adventure of the soul.

There are three stages of increasing depth, which have their place in the progress of the soul in any types of creative life, and obviously they are significant for our purpose here.

(1) There must be *concentration* for any great achievement. That is an essential discipline. Concentration means the organization of all one's mental powers for the specific task in hand. Random and distracting tendencies must be overcome by the expulsive power of one absorbing interest. Training in concentration is the first step toward any difficult goal in life.

(2) *Meditation* is simply concentration in a special field. It is concentration of one's mental powers upon a spiritual object, aim, or aspiration. It has often been called "recollection," which does not mean remembering. It means the unification of all one's inward capacities upon a single focus point of thought or aspiration. There must be absolute dominion over wayward impulses and wandering thoughts. This does call for special and serious discipline.

(3) *Contemplation* is the highest stage of concentration. The mind is no longer focused upon a specific object, idea, or aim. It is like the highest moment in the enjoyment of music, or in the presence of surprising beauty, or in the rapture of love. Consciousness is no longer differentiated into the duality of *subject* over against *object.* It feels as though it had entered the stream of life itself, is being borne along in the flowing current of it, and finds its life in that larger enveloping Life. There comes a quickening and vivification of the unfathomable depth of the soul. Its subsoil wealth is set free. There is an intense unification of all the powers of the spirit with a release of energy and a state of glowing expectation. It is activity, not passivity, but activity fused with the peace and serenity of receptivity. And with it comes an unmistakable and formidable spiritual power—a power which flows out of complete unification and concentration.

Chapter III

THE INNER LIFE AND THE SOCIAL ORDER

Some time ago in the Chapel of the University of Chicago, Charles Clayton Morrison, Editor of the *Christian Century,* preached a challenging sermon at the Pastors' Institute in that city. He began his sermon with the statement that Christianity now stands at the crisis of its entire history. That crisis, he asserted, has emerged out of the fact that Christianity is now shifting the centre of its gravity from the inner life to the social community. The speaker contended that, in the past, religion has derived its vitality from the private experience of individual men and women; it is now discovering the religious resources that have lain hidden in the wide field of the social order. In the past the religious transactions which were believed to take place in the inner life between God and the soul were transactions "in an ethical vacuum." Religion of this former type was occupied with the subjectivities of the inner life, it was busy with "its abstractions and fantasies and ideologies," and was unable to pass over from the inner life "into the burly world outside."

A religious experience, he held, which originates in

the inner life tends to become a private luxury and lacks the disposition to take control and direction of large-scale movements and events in the public order of the world. The shift of the centre of gravity now taking place, he said, is away from *the primacy of the inner life* as the field of a valid and creative religion over to *the primacy of a social vision,* out of which a real inner life may spring. "The present crisis then in Christianity," he declared, "arises from the necessity of finding the foundations of religion in the world of human society conceived as the Kingdom of God."

There can, I think, be little question that Christianity today is facing a momentous crisis, though I am too familiar with the numerous crises of its past history to accept without further debate the conclusion that it is *the* crisis *par excellence.* In any case I am profoundly convinced that the above diagnosis of the cause and occasion for this present crisis is an inadequate one. The situation in the religious world is far too complex to be squeezed down to a single shift of the centre of gravity. We are still in the swirl of the mighty currents of the incompleted Renaissance, and the entire basis of the significance, the validity and the authority of religion has for some time now been undergoing an acid test. We have outgrown to a large extent the doll stage of religious life with its enjoyment of pictorial imagery, magic, and the dim magnificence of mythology and superstitious creations. We have left behind, with the discarded Ptolemaic astronomy, the vivid conceptions of a sky-dome heaven and a literal subterranean hell.

It is not easy to overestimate the mental effect which has been occasioned by the loss of this vivid pictorial imagery through which most persons for two thousand years have formed for themselves "the scenery and circumstance of the newly parted soul." Much that was real and vital in religious thought only a little while ago now seems to us like intolerable babyism, and it has dropped away forever from our minds, as our baby clothes have done from our bodies. But these discarded ideas which our growing knowledge has pushed off were the slow growth of the racial life of the world. They formed the psychological climate of many generations. They had become comfortable with long habit, and they furnished a cultural atmosphere of faith that made it easy to breathe and act as though religion were a normal, natural function of life.

We of modern times have been stripped of the comfortable clothing which our ancestors found so convenient. That cultural atmosphere of theirs does not fit our minds. A mighty transition has passed over the world and left it forever altered. And we happen to be living at a time when the old order is dead and the new order is not yet quite born. We have shed the literal, the pictorial, the mythological imagery of religious life and we have not yet created a spiritual cultural atmosphere in which we breathe and live with natural ease as our forebears did.

We have not, furthermore, quite succeeded in passing over from external authorities, imposed from without, to inward compulsions, which work as silently and yet as powerfully as do those invisible forces which hold the earth in its journey round the sun. The Renaissance, now more than five hundred years in extent, will not be over and finished until these *new birth processes* have come to fruition and man has found those springs of life and faith which fit his new stages of intellectual growth. Among the changes of attitude that will mark the new birth of religion there will certainly be an immensely increased emphasis on the redemption of society as the true organ of the Kingdom of God, but that will be only one feature, however important a feature, of a newly created religious faith which fits the world-order of the new time.

My next observation in reference to the sermon under consideration is that there never has been any genuine religion of the inner life which operated in "an ethical vacuum," except possibly in the primitive stages of religion and ethics. Religion and ethics have always developed together in the closest intimacy of interaction. They probably, however, do not have the same psychological origin. One does not spring out of the other. There is no use arguing which has the primacy, which is Jacob and which is Esau, for they are in their own nature quite unique and *sui generis* attitudes, as irreducible into terms of anything else as is the appreciation of beauty.

Religion in its original unique form is the soul's attitude, response and adjustment, in the presence of what are felt to be supreme realities of a transcendent order. Ethics in its essential meaning has to do with that strange attitude which we express by the words, "I ought," and with the *right* adjustment of life within a society of men and women. They are alike in the fact that both have their ground in man's fundamental capacity to expand life in ideal directions and to live out beyond what is presented to the senses as fact. There would be no use of *ought* if one could be satisfied with *what is,* and there would be no awe and wonder, no "numinous" state of mind, if we were mere calm spectators of passing phenomena. They both attach to that sphere of life in us that has been called "imaginative dominion over experience."

Religion springs out of our faith, which often amounts to discovery, that there is a divine Overworld with which we have dealings, while ethics moves in the horizontal sphere of human society, but always at the same time implies a faith, amounting often to compelling vision, that actions that *ought to be done* will enlarge the scope of both individual and social life. There can be no significant ethics without ideal vision of a life that *ought* to be. They both have to do with a *beyond,* in one case with an eternal world which already is as it ought to be; in the other case with an imperfect temporal world which can be made by human effort more nearly like what ought to be.

The story of the sublimation of religion under the influence of the growth and historical process of ethical ideals is the story of one of the most impressive achievements which man has yet made on the earth. In its primitive stage the element of fear in religion was very great. It was never true, as the Roman poet Lucretius thought, that "fear created the gods," but it is a fact that man in his childhood was much more impressed with the *power* of unseen beings above him than with their goodness or their friendliness and their intention to bless and help. Religion in its primitive form, as Bergson has put it, was the cradle in which the race in its infancy rocked itself to sleep from its fears and terrors.

Little by little in the slow stages of expanding social life man discovered the immense significance of human love and the worth of moral goodness, both in itself and in its creative social effects. It gradually dawned upon him, too, that what had seemed at first like sternness or anger in men's dealings with one another was often only a way of training and discipline for the making of a better person. It is an immemorial discovery of parents that young and immature lives cannot be guided into the formation of wisdom and stability of character alone by soft and easy methods. There must be agencies of restraint in the great business of moral guidance. Men came, through such experiences, to see, even if only dimly, that the strongest and most effective persons were, after all, the persons who had been trained by severe discipline. Through his ethical discoveries of the social significance of love, the worth of goodness and the value of discipline in the sphere of his own life, man began to refashion his thoughts and ideals of the beings above him who controlled and guided his destiny. He saw them now through the imaginative ethical forms of what was the highest and best that he knew in his own world of experience.

The most momentous step in the process of sublimation came through the insight that human life continues after death in another sphere and that the divine beings above are moral guardians of those higher issues of destiny. That *insight* throws back much light upon the transcendent quality of man's mind, even in the early dawning stages of life, and it is, of course, a nice question how far the original insight had its birth in the sphere of what may be called religious experience, and how far it was the outgrowth of ethical ideals of an animistic type. We do not need to stop and debate that question now. It is clear enough in any case that when once the insight was reached ethical ideals from that time on worked powerfully upon religious conceptions. The divine beings were thought of not merely as embodiments of capricious power but as the keepers of the issues of life and death.

It was an epoch in the life of the race when the faith was born that the moral gains of life are conserved and, under the guardianship of divine beings, determine man's future destiny. When that discovery was made the long process of casting out *fear* with *love* was well under way. I have obviously presented here the higher constructive aspect of this insight of the conservation of personality and have omitted to speak of the burden and drag which utilitarian conceptions of the future life have often been to human progress. As I write this I have just seen a shaft of light break through the clouds and make one glorious spot of radiance on the sea, while all the rest of the surrounding sea lay dark in shadow. So it has often been with man's noblest insights. A shaft of illumination throws a sudden gleam of light, revealing in a flash man's divine possibilities, while the main stream of life runs on untouched by the glory.

Not less powerfully has religion influenced the development of the ethical life of man. There has always been interaction, osmosis, between these two supreme values of life. If ethics with its ideals has sublimated religion, religion at the same time has brought steadiness, fortification and an *élan* of marching power to man's ethical life. It is quite impossible to conceive what our life would have been if it had been deprived of the faiths which religion has brought to birth in us. We make our risky ventures for ideal ends with very little empirical evidence that they will lead to triumph. Anybody who engages in moral battles is as familiar with defeats as he is with victories. Frustration is one of the most common experiences of life. What we care for most as a goal to be attained often seems to be at the mercy of a trivial or capricious happening. If we had no assurances except those which our senses and our memories give us, we should have a feeble armor for the supreme battles of life to which we feel summoned.

Religion whenever it has been at its best has brought the steadiness of a wider reference. We can bear the tragedy of present frustration or of momentary defeat if we have inward assurance enough that eternal forces are allied with us for the cause that is *good*. Religion has in the main brought this vision of expectation. It has contributed the faith that the deepest nature of things is morally grounded and is there behind the lonely fighter for what is right. It has brought confidence to man that the eternal Heart of the universe backs his moral endeavors and that in the long run— the run is sometimes very long—in the long run what ought to be is what will be.

Religious faith at its highest has brought the conviction that our God Himself is an Emmanuel God and has entered the darkly colored stream of history, partakes of the sorrows and tragedies of the temporal order and treads the winepress with us even when it is reddest, and that we are never alone when we are striving upward. It fortifies us with the hope that we can in some sense become organs of His divine purpose and be revealing places for His will to break into manifestation. In fact, too, religion furnishes to ethics its richest and most adequate goal of life. It heartens us with the belief that we are most completely ourselves when we are nearest in spirit and character to the pattern of life which the Christian religion presents and that we are most truly at the goal of human life when we approximate most closely to the nature of the God whom we worship.

In the light of this constant interaction between religion and ethics, I maintain that it is an historically untenable position to claim that an inner religious experience is "bound to exist without reference to the public social world outside." It is quite possible that theological conceptions—what Dr. Morrison loves to call "ideologies"—may come to be ends in themselves, in fact they have no doubt frequently come to be ends in themselves and have lulled the smug and satisfied soul to rest with the existing social *status quo*—"the mess we's in"—but I seriously doubt whether *vital inward religion* has ever done it.

I mean by "vital inward religion" an actual personal contact with the central eternal Stream of Life. He says that "the first Christians derived their inner experience from their social vision." I believe that is a misreading of the facts. What happened in the first instance was a fresh discovery of God, a breaking in of Eternity into the life of men—"we have beheld His glory," they say, and forthwith all the ethical values of life were altered. These men did not originate the idea of the Kingdom of God, nor did their Master himself originate it, it was the slow growth of centuries, but their new vision of God and the throbbing experience of His life in their lives recast the entire meaning of the Kingdom and brought to them a burning passion for its coming as a realm of love and brotherhood—"righteousness, peace and joy in the holy Spirit."

Dr. Morrison has much to say of the social sterility of "evangelicalism," in which, as he says, the doctrine of the new birth holds a central place. But here once more he is talking about a congealed system and not about a vital inward experience. One of the most dynamic things the modern world has seen was that same evangelical movement in the days when it *moved*, with its original high *caloric*. It came like a vernal equinox into the morally dull and static life of the eighteenth century. It turned water to wine, it brought prodigals home, it raised life out of death. It produced miracles of transformation. But the most remarkable thing about it was the freshly inspired social impulse which it produced. It reformed prisons, it stopped the

slave trade, it freed slaves. It made its converts un-
comfortable over wrong social conditions. It sent mis-
sionaries to create hospitals and to conquer ignorance
in almost every land on the globe. It was always as
much outward as it was inward, though its creative
spring was assuredly a birth of new life from the central Source of Life.

It is surely an exaggeration to say, as was said in this
sermon, that "after nineteen centuries of Christianity's
presence in the world the brutalities of the secular
social system have not been radically mitigated." If the
writer of that sentence could make an excursion into
almost any previous century of the nineteen past ones
he would pine to return to the one in which he lives.
And the contrast that would strike him most as he came
back would be the fact that nearly everybody in the
former centuries took the "brutalities" as a matter of
course, as a settled feature of a "wrecked and fallen
world," as a *datum* of foreordination, whereas almost
no inwardly alive Christian feels that way today in
reference to the secular social system. Something new
has happened. *We* are determined to remake the social
world and we *expect* to remake it. That is a fact of
major importance.

I have spent most of my life studying mystical religion and its exponents. It reveals in its long history a
large amount of psychical abnormality, a good-sized
element of doubtful metaphysical theory, and more

than one likes to see of "gullibility." But there remains over and above the liabilities a great central nucleus of extraordinary religious experience through which men and women have found themselves raised to an irresistible consciousness of contact with God. They have felt through that experience as though the Ocean of Eternal Life had surged into the tiny inlet of their being. This experience of rising into the Eternal Life has again and again brought with it a marvelous increase of vitality and power for the individual to live by. To use William James' phrase it has turned them into "human dynamos." It does not of course take them out of the social and intellectual environment of their time and give them supernaturally the outlook, the ideals and the social patterns of epochs not yet born. Even St. Francis with all his social passion struggled on with thirteenth-century economic and social ideas. But what does happen, what has happened, to these persons whose inner life has been vivified and quickened, is that they begin at once to feel a passion for the enrichment and enlargement of the lives of others. They say with almost one accord that no vision of God is adequate which remains private and is not translated into life and action. The true test of an inner vision, they all insist, is the impact it gives toward pushing back the skirts of darkness and making the area of the Kingdom of God wider.

It is true that "the kingdoms of this world are still

the kingdoms of *this world*." But as soon as one studies the history of Christianity minutely he discovers that the main-line stream of Christianity through the centuries has not been concerned with Christ's ethics, has hardly been aware indeed that he brought a new ethic. The gaze has been fixed on a supernatural Being from another world whose mission here was to bring a way of *redemption* and to found a mysterious Church as the authoritative instrument of it.

The hymn which I used to sing with enthusiasm in my early Christian experience,

> *Hallelujah! 'tis done*
> *I believe in the Son;*
> *I am saved by the blood*
> *Of the crucified One,*

expresses quite accurately what Christianity has in general meant to men. The focus of attention has been on a supernatural nativity, a crucifixion of agony and death and a supernatural resurrection and ascension. The theology of the Church has been built around those doctrines, the art of the Church has glorified those features of its faith. One looked in vain and listened in vain until recent times in the historic Church for the proclamation of a way of life which involves the practice of the Galilean gospel. It has been in the main the mystic and the heretic who have endeavored to *restore* primitive Christianity as a way of life among men. The social gospel is for most persons a new discovery. Furthermore the affiliation of the Church with the State has of course always tended to secularize Christianity and to make the Sermon on the Mount seem to be an utterly foreign, if not a fantastic, group of ideas. We are very young in the faith that Christianity is something to be *done,* not something to be recited, or used as a scheme to insure heavenly joy. Give us a little more time!

It should be added, I think, that there is no magic in that phrase "social gospel." It is no easy matter to settle offhand precisely what was the ethics of Jesus. It is one of the most acute problems of New Testament scholarship. But even if it were as plain and clear as is the ethics of John Dewey we should still be confronted with grave difficulties. It is never possible to pick up an ethical system and lift it out of its temporal setting and local habitat and put it down unaltered upon a world of new complexities and wholly altered civilization. What has to be done if Christ's ethics is to be effective is to reincarnate the spirit that was in the founder of this way of life, to recapture his faith in God and man and to live in the dominion and power of a love like his.

My final trouble with the sermon in question lies in its insistence on the *primacy of social vision* in the sphere of religion. We are, it tells us, to put the social vision first and then to get an inner life to match it.

Chapter IV

THE FUNDAMENTAL GROUND OF RELIGION IN MAN

An exuberant French philosopher a generation ago affirmed that "man is incurably religious." If he meant to say that all bipeds that possess a face which can smile and speak intelligible words are *ipso facto* "incurably religious" he was undoubtedly wrong. It is quite possible to be an unfeathered biped with broad, flat nails, to smile and talk, even to argue logically in syllogisms, and yet to be wholly free from the tendency to make a religious response. It is obvious that when Auguste Sabatier used the word "incurably," he had no thought of implying that religion is an abnormal condition of life, from which one needs to be "cured." He was merely using a vivid phrase to affirm that a fullfledged person, with all his capacities opened out, with the powers of his life brought to full bloom, essentially has that attitude of spirit, that response to a Beyond, which we name by the word "religion."

Religion is a vague word with a vast range of meanings. The Latin derivation of the word throws almost no light upon the central significance of religious experience. The word, as we use it today, covers the entire gamut of the characteristic attitudes of religion, from a low, coarse emotional "adjustment" to powers felt to be important for life-interests, up to a pure, lofty spiritual surmise of unseen reality and a quiet consciousness of "belonging" to an eternal realm of life and being. It may have a large factor of fear at its root, as is often the case in the primitive stage, or it may be spiritualized and sublimated to a state of purity that casts out fear and leaves it utterly behind.

Historically and psychologically speaking, religion has been one of the three supreme driving forces in the life of the human race. The quest for food, expanding into the acquisitive desire for possession; passionate interest in the opposite sex, which on its highest level we call "love"; and the adjustment, or joyous response, to supersensuous realities that are believed to be important for the fullness of life—these are the three supreme springs of activity, the three fundamental sources of anxiety and joy in the life of man as we know him here on the earth. The first two of these springs, or "urges" of life, are so obviously instinctive and "natural," so plainly biologically engendered, that they hardly seem to demand any elaborate philosophical interpretation.

This third great *élan* of life, however, has always seemed mysterious. Here is something more than a biological trait; something more than a "natural" urge. Here somehow "the finger of God" seems to be im-

plied. Here if anywhere is where "grace" breaks in.
And yet the *function* of religion has frequently been
questioned, its validity has been doubted and its origin
and genesis have long been in debate. What makes
man a religious being? is a question which in ages of
enlightenment we are bound to ask, though the answer
strangely lags.

For Kant, religion is a corollary to our *moral* nature.
We are religious because we are inherently moral beings. God is for us a necessary postulate of the Moral
Will, which Kant called Practical Reason. The Moral
Will in Kant's thought is a primary, basic, essential
feature of a rational person. It towers even above pure
reason in man and holds the primacy in the inner realm
of our being. It is autonomous, that is, self-legislative,
and in its own right of eminent domain it issues an
absolute command of duty which Kant calls a *categorical imperative,* or universal law of moral action. This
overwhelming call within man which says uncondi-
tionally, "Thou must," at once implies that *we can do
what must be done,* we *can* because we *ought.* Emerson
has caught the grandeur of this august inward call in
his well-known lines:

> *When duty whispers low, "thou must,"*
> *The youth replies, "I can."*

In other lines equally familiar Emerson speaks of the
absolute character of this inward imperative by the

phrase, "a voice without reply," a call which leaves no alternatives.

We are, therefore, Kant insisted, rationally justified in postulating, that is, in assuming as real, everything the non-existence of which would make imperative moral action, the ethical life, impossible. Kant then proceeds to show that God, by which he means a rational, spiritual Order in the universe which backs the moral deed and which in the long run makes moral adventures *intelligible,* is an absolutely essential condition of a Moral Will. If this universe of ours is to be a sphere for moral personality then God must be real, or at least the moral adventurer must act on the *faith* that He is real. Otherwise our moral insights would prove to be mere empty buzzings in our own head, and would land us in hopeless confusions amidst the blank walls of a universe completely sterile of moral import. The faith, therefore, which makes religion possible for Kant springs out of this primary moral nature of man as a necessary feature to it. Religion consequently on this basis has its ground in the moral deeps of man's being.

There can be no question, I think, that the moral and religious aspects of man's life are closely akin to one another. But those who know most about the scope and significance of religion from inward personal experience of it do not feel satisfied to make it dependent upon something other than itself, even upon something as sublime as the categorical imperative, nor can they consent to have it reduced to a postulate, to an implication, which gives it a secondary status—the position of a concubine like Hagar, not that of a true bride and consort like Sarah. It is another way, a roundabout way to be sure, of considering religion to be an *addendum* to human nature, not an inherent, essential and fundamental expression of normal human personality. Kant has supplied us with important clues which point the way to the true ground of our highest spiritual values, but his way of making the journey to the City of the Soul is not, I am convinced, the best way to it.

One serious trouble with Kant's theory of religion is that it confines religion within the restricted bounds of reason. It is possible, no doubt, to expand the word "reason" and to make it include, as it should do, attitudes and values of life. Kant himself sometimes raises reason to its true concrete consecration, but the word tends for the most part to stand for cold, abstract speculation. The result is that by this treatment religion becomes "rationalized" in the well-known manner of the eighteenth century. It becomes too far sundered from man's emotional and practical life. It lacks the throb and thrust of the full reality of life. It does not take its place in the sphere of actual experience. It remains something to be argued about, not something warm and intimate with its own vital breath of life. It is distant and secondary, it comes at the end of a syllogism, or, in any case, it is at the mercy of a postulate. The consequence is that we find ourselves talking in terms of a divided self. "Reason" is thought of as isolated, almost insulated, from the emotions. "Reason" and "emotions" on this treatment belong in separate compartments of man's life. They do not keep house together coöperatively. They always haunt the divorce court. The will, even the exalted moral will, is treated as an entity "apart" in its own private domain. It becomes "debased" the moment it has fellowship with, or is influenced by, the emotional member of this divided household.

The reaction from this attempt to find religion solely within the bounds of "reason," led directly to many varying attempts to discover another ground of religion. On the one hand its origin is traced to the *feelings*. Then again, another school finds it in the *will*, thought of as a native urge, as an adjustment process of life. But religion cannot legitimately be reduced to the function of any *one* compartment of our complicated nature, nor in fact can that "complicated nature" itself, as we now know, be cut up into fragmentary parts, carrying on their several functions in isolation, as divided kingdoms, or like the tetrarchies of the Herods. Kant himself, too often unconscious of the full significance of what he was doing, prepared the way toward the discovery of the unified self, the indivisible oneness of the central life of the normal person.

That central unity of man's inner life must be the point of departure from which all our trails of exploration emerge. A self which deliquesced into a spray of conscious atoms, or one which dissipated into a shower of shot, could experience no *identities,* could hold to no permanent *values* of life, and consequently could know nothing of what we mean by religion of a spiritual type. The unity of a self-conscious person is one of the most unique, as it is one of the most amazing facts to be found in a universe which at most points seems to be a sum of parts. In endeavoring to account for religion we shall do well to look for its ground in this central unity of the self. Religion must not be reduced to a speculation of "reason," nor to a "feeling" of dependence, nor to a "way of life-adjustment," for it is something which our entire unified and integral self is and feels and does.

Rudolf Otto has put all contemporary religious students into his debt through his extremely important book, *Das Heilige,* which has been admirably translated into English under the title, *The Idea of the Holy.* Otto insists on the primacy of religion. He is convinced that it is utterly unique, *ausserordentlich, sui generis.* It cannot be analyzed into derivative elements, or reduced to anything else. It is not based on a postulate. It is not an *addendum* to human nature. It does not stand in dependence on something else. It does not rest for its right of being upon the sense of *ought.* It stands in its own sovereign right. It has its own sphere of inward compulsion and it is inexplicable in terms of anything but itself. It breaks into expression as a state of wonder mingled with awe and reverent fear. There is in the religious consciousness a mysterious sense of something more than is visible, a Presence deeply interfused, a *numinous Beyond,* which throws the beholder into a peculiar state of mind unlike any other known state. It is a strange fusion of joy and awe, of thrill and hush. Edmund Spenser coined the phrase, "my dear dread," to express his attitude of joy and at the same time of restraint in the presence of his wife. She was his "dear dread." That feeling of "dear dread," raised to a higher level, expresses this sense of the *numinous.*

Everyone who remembers at all vividly his childhood will recall experiences of "dear dread"—a haunting feeling of Something *there,* behind the seen, which both attracts and disturbs. W. H. Hudson in his autobiographical book, *Far Away and Long Ago,* has given some striking experiences of this sort, which came to him when he was alone in the presence of moving scenes of nature. "I used to steal out of the house," he says, "alone when the moon was at its full, to stand, silent and motionless, near some group of large trees, gazing at the dusky green foliage silvered by the beams; and at such times the mystery would grow until a sensation of delight would change to one of fear and the fear increase until it was no longer to be borne and I would hastily escape, to recover the sense of reality and safety indoors."

Browning's line, "The child feels God a moment," expresses exactly those sudden flashes of awe and wonder, that sense of "something more" above, beyond, within, which makes the unseen seem as real as the things that are seen and touched. There is on such occasions a flooding, overbrimming, palpitating burst of enlargement and joy, but, interfused with it, the awe which comes in the presence of a *mysterium tremendum,* a divine Other, a reality wholly unlike the well-known finite things of ordinary experience.

This trait of human nature by which we have these numinous experiences is a *datum,* an ultimate fact, like the experience of beauty, or like the compulsion of ought, not to be explained in terms of anything else. We are *made that way.* We have numinous experiences —as we have the unanalyzable taste of sweetness—and these experiences make us religious beings. Religion is not something to argue about; it is something to feel happening in an overbrimming state of "dear dread."

Professor Otto has given a most impressive interpretation of his position in his book, which I have interpreted in my own way. No brief account of it can do anything like justice to it. To be fully appreciated it must be read in the calm, luminous, persuasive words of the noble scholar who originated this "numinous" interpretation of religion. I am convinced that he has made a permanent and significant contribution to the actual *process* of religion. The aspect of awe and wonder, of mysterious dread and reverent joy in the presence of the Beyond breaking in upon the soul cannot well be minimized. The overbrimming life and the palpitating heart are undoubtedly features of all genuine religion.

But, once more, we are left here with only one aspect of religion brought into emphasis. This time it is the "non-rational" aspect which receives especial emphasis, and there *is* unmistakably a non-rationalizable aspect to religion. Religion is rightly declared to be unique, but in this account of it, it forever remains a mysterious experience in the presence of a Something tremendous but unknown; Something awe-inspiring but inexplicable. So far as we are here told anything explicit, it is in terms of *feelings* which stir our being. We are thrown into a moved state. We palpitate, we overbrim. But we *know* no more about the Object which moved us than we did before we were moved. It is and remains a *mysterium tremendum*. We have felt a Presence which disturbs us with joy and wonder. But it remains an unknown Beyond. It is wholly Other. It is not revealed or revealable. It does not raise our human life to a new intelligible significance, since we know no more about what is ultimately real than we did before. The numinous experience does not bring the whole of our life into play. It does not at once inform the mind, stir the emotional deeps in us and fortify the will, as religion in its fullness should do.

For more than a generation now we have been passing through a period marked by attempts to explain religion psychologically. Hume with manifest genius pointed out the way more than a century and a half ago. This psychological method of explanation at once gave promise of yielding rich returns. Hopes and expectations from its researches were very high. Those of us who were young at the time when the new wave of psychology swept over the modern world a generation ago believed that we were on the frontiers of new realms of life and thought about to be explored. We stood like "stout Cortez," silent on our peak, as we waited for the latest news which the psychologists were sure to bring us about the unfathomable reaches of the soul. But we were quickly doomed to disappointment and disillusionment. What "stout Cortez" or, more correctly, the real discoverer Balboa, would have found if he had realistically dealt with the situation which confronted him as he "looked at the Pacific" from his "peak in Darien," would have been just interminable stretches of salt water, and then more salt water beyond that. The far-beyond that seemed so vague and poetic would turn out to be the same thing as the commonplace water near the shore. "Leagues and leagues beyond these leagues there is more sea," but it is after all only a matter of addition, not a new revelation.

So, too, what the psychologists found when they proceeded to explore the soul realistically, that is to say scientifically, was a very wide range of conscious processes, with a new process following on after each passing one. But it was all of the same *order*. Nothing new and novel dawned. There was no way to get beyond the series of successive processes. There was no way by this realistic method to rise to a new level or to find a new frontier. There was nothing in evidence but the old flat stretch of empirical processes, continued *ad libitum*. It soon became manifest that the psychologist had no magic, no wizardry, by which he could work miracles for us in this inner realm of ours. He could open no gates into a region beyond the series of mental phenomena. The psychologist was doomed to observe the soul from the outside and thus never really to find it.

Some of the more "soft" and genial psychologists, like Frederic W. Myers and William James, did try to comfort us with the suggestion that the mind has a deep subcellar below the footlights of consciousness, where mysterious events might happen, a subliminal zone in which the bubbling springs of religion might well be allowed to bubble. They conceived like Kubla that

The sacred river ran
Through caverns measureless to man.

But it did not take very long to discover that the subliminal zone, like subtropical ones, had hissing serpents as well as glorious birds of paradise. It might be a gateway to unexplored regions of heavenly joys, but it also opened on "the foam of perilous seas." If it admitted celestial visitants, it indiscriminately also let in a medley brood of visitors from less favored abodes. There is undoubted wealth hidden away in the subsoil regions within us, below the threshold of consciousness, but we cannot yet, if ever, leap forthwith to the sound conclusion that God is assuredly most at home in regions which we cannot at present explore.

To return, however, to the realistic method of psychology we can see easily why it was bound to fail to bring an adequate answer to questions about the nature and origin of religion. Psychology, in its legitimate field can deal only with *mental phenomena,* i.e., with passing states and processes which appear in consciousness. It neither asks, nor expects to answer, questions that are concerned with ultimate realities or issues. If religion were due solely to the functions of a peculiar human instinct, or if it were synonymous with a distinct emotion, then psychology could throw a flood of light upon it in terms of exact description. And psychologists have searched patiently and persistently for such appropriate genetic instincts and emotions. But religion in its essential nature cannot be reduced to instinctive urges or to emotional reactions. There is something more, there is a residue, which will not yield to such description.

There is, furthermore, another difficulty inherent in the psychological method. By a necessary limitation of this method psychology as such can deal adequately only with the subjective side of experience, with what passes in a mental series before the observing spectator. There is no bridge from within to without, from here to yonder. There is no way of getting out of the "ego-centric predicament." Religion for psychology is bound to stay humbly on the ground and be content to remain a manward affair. It is a "one-way road." The tracks and the traffic are all in one direction and on one level. There are yearnings and strivings to be reported. There is the will-to-believe, there are projections, rainbow hopes, wish-thoughts, expectant dreams, visions of compensations for the disappointments and frustrations of life, but psychology knows of no bridge-span which goes across from the subjective side to objective and verifiable realities.

Psychology would cease to be a scientific branch of study if it should leave its field of observation and description and should launch out into the deep waters of metaphysical interpretation. When we pass from the level of observed facts of consciousness to an interpretation in terms of significance and value and the *objective validity* of experience, we have gone beyond the scientific method. It may, therefore, be taken as settled that psychologies of religion will always stop short of any type of religion that can meet man's deepest religious needs, since psychologies of religion have reached their limit when they have dealt with observed processes, subjective urges, in a word, with religious *phenomena,* and these fall far short of what we mean by *religion. Religion is essentially constituted by the conscious relationship of a personal self in vital correspondence with some sort of Objective Reality.*

We should no more expect to find God, or a World of supersensuous reality, in a psychological laboratory than we should expect to find Him through a telescope in an astronomical observatory, or than we should expect to find Him by scaling Olympus or Mt. Everest. Unless we are to assume that God is an observable object, we need not look for Him with the instruments and methods of any empirical science, though all sciences present clues which point toward the great Reality. The God we should "find" by that sort of search would be a finite god—a god in space and time —not an eternal Being.

Is there any reality within our sphere which transcends time and space, and which thus may be a gateway of approach to a World of supersensuous reality such as we demand for genuine religion? Yes, there is. The knowing self within us by whatever name it is called—mind, soul, self-as-knower, I myself, or central personality—belongs to a different order from that of observed phenomena. Plato made the point very clear in his day, and his greatest disciples have enlarged upon it, that the mind, the soul, what he called the *nous* in us, which organizes the facts of experience, the *data* of experience, and interprets them by means of universal and permanent forms of thought cannot itself at the same time be *one of the facts to be experienced*. The *nous* in us must have had its origin in, and must belong to, a higher World Order, the World of Nous—Spirit.

Plato was always inclined to suggest the lofty origin and the exalted status of the soul in mythological parables which easily mislead literal-minded readers, but the central point is plain enough in the *Dialogues* which deal with knowledge, that the mind, or soul, beholds by virtue of its own nature eternal realities, interprets sense-data in the light of the eternal forms which are native to it, and itself belongs to that higher World Order, which Plato calls *the noumenal World, the World of Being,* which is the only possible basis of *Truth*. A mind that can rise above fleeting appearances which are presented to sense, and through these thick veils can apprehend *truth* and *beauty* and *the eternally good,* is itself already a denizen of that higher World where these things are "real presences," and is a participator in them. We should, no doubt, tell this in different words today, but the truth remains essentially as this ancient prophet of the soul set it forth in the Academe twenty-four hundred years ago.

One of our most common blunders is that of treating
the mind as though it were only a spectator. There is,
however, in beings of our type no real mind that is
merely a spectator-mind—no mind that merely "receives" and "observes" presented facts. Every mind
which deserves that name unifies, organizes and *interprets* everything that is presented to it. There is, therefore, something presupposed in the nature of mind
which did not come from outside nor arise out of
change and process. Change and process are facts *for
it,* not the ground of its being. "Time and space" which
are the basis of change and process are forms of the
mind through which it arranges its world of experience
in place and in succession. Every attempt to derive
space and time *from* experience tacitly already presupposes consciousness of space and time. The little child
who asked, "Mummie, where's yesterday gone and
what's tomorrow doing now?" already was feeling the
necessity for a transcendental deduction of time. Whatever else, and whatever more, space and time may be,
they *must* be original forms, or potential capacities, of
the mind itself.

It is no less true that the necessity for causal relation,
which pertains to all our interpretations of events, must
have its origin and basis in the fundamental nature of
the knowing, organizing, mind. The causal relation between phenomena is never a perceived fact, but even
if it were a perceived fact, no number of instances of

the perception of a causal connection would enable us to leap to the conclusion that every event *must* have a cause. *Must,* wherever it emerges, goes beyond any possible experience of sense. The mind that organizes facts with the coercion of *must* has added something to the mere bare "facts" themselves.

There is, furthermore, a unity to the knowing mind, as I have already said, which no observed facts in the outside world can fully account for. There is nothing like it in the world of relativity, and there is nothing outside itself which can explain it. The kind of mind which is essential for what we mean by knowledge, by truth, the mind which imposes its universal and necessary forms upon all that it knows, has no counterpart anywhere in the world of process and relativity. It is a unique reality. It belongs to a different order.

This unique mind, which we have been considering, not only organizes the facts of experience under universal forms and imposes the aspect of *must* upon what is known, but it goes beyond everything which sense reports as given fact, and anticipates by imaginative forecast what is to be, but is not yet. The mind may by a flash of insight, by a stroke of genius, announce a law of nature which in its operation reaches far beyond all observed facts and which determines in advance of further perception whole vast areas of facts and events in regions not yet explored. Something similar is true in the realm of ideal goodness, and, again, in the realm of creative art. Ethical insight may enable a person to anticipate a form and type of goodness that never has actually been before, but now is made real in this actual world, through this man's creative ideal. So, too, the synoptic mind of an artist may produce a beautiful creation which transcends in unity and harmony any object that has previously existed in the world of things.

Not every imaginative insight, of course, in any of these fields proves to be *creative*. There are aesthetic and ethical "duds," which have no perduring worth, as there are "duds" among explosive shells. There are two types of ideals which are totally unlike each other. There are (1) ideals which are capricious projections of the mind, effervescent day-dreams, vague yearnings. They are subjective "sports" and have no rootage in the eternal nature of things. They are capricious. They are shot out at random and the universe declines to *back* them or to give them validity.

The other type of ideal (2) is of quite another quality. A genuine creative ideal is an imaginative forecast of possibilities that have their ground in the total world order to which our minds intimately belong. An ideal of this second type has been prepared for by the structure of the universe, by the slow stages of historical development and by the fitting aptitudes of the mind of the idealist who has the vision. It is the "more yet," dimly prophesied by the curve of the arc of events already projected. It bursts on the mind of the creative idealist somewhat as new and higher peaks break in on the sight of the mountain climber as he reaches new levels of his ascent. The creator of ideals of this second type sees in advance what must be in order to complete and fulfill what already is. He forecasts what is involved in the nature of things as the astronomer surmises the new planet by the observed variations of those already known, or as the lover of beauty *sees* how an uncompleted work of art must be finished to fulfill the lines of harmony already laid down. Here there is nothing capricious, nothing left to chance, nothing aimlessly shot out of a pistol. The new coheres with the old. It adds a new unit of growth, a fresh ring of increase, and one is not surprised to find that the eternal nature of things *backs* the creative mind of the lonely idealist as he makes his brave adventure. We calmly say, "How otherwise?"

What I am leading up to is the point that minds of this type—and we all possess some of this organizing and creative capacity—go beyond *what is,* surmise *the more yet,* transcend *the given,* have the inward power to see the invisible and to *live* in correspondence with a Beyond which is absolutely real. Beings of that scope and range are something more than "forked radishes with heads fantastically carved," or "unfeathered bipeds with broad flat nails." They partake of another order, another level of reality to that of the biological series. They are spiritual beings. They belong in a noumenal order and have correspondence with an Over-world, in spite of the fact that they have visible bodies with avoirdupois weight, that they consume food and often do foolish things.

Not only do these minds of ours expand life in ideal directions and go beyond what is, but at their best these ideals of ours correlate and correspond with some sort of objective reality. They advance truth. They set forward the march of goodness. Through coöperation with God they build a new stage of the Kingdom of God in the world. We are in that respect not dreamers; we are actual builders. We exercise a dominion over events. We carry the ball on toward the goal. Something not ourselves co-works with us, as the currents of the ocean co-work with the mariner who is traveling in their direction. Something more than our finite will pushes behind our effort. Something large and luminous backs our deeds. When we are on right lines of advance doors open before us. We find ourselves in coöperative union with a larger Mind and a wiser Will. We have sound reason to believe that what is highest in us is deepest in the nature of things. We become organs of a spiritual kingdom and stand in vital relation to an Eternal Mind and Heart and Will with whom we coöperate.

There is something in us and of us that did not originate in the world of matter, in the time-space order, in the phenomenal process. We are more than curious bits of the earth's crust, more than biological exhibits. We have a spiritual lineage. We may have collateral connections with flat-nosed baboons, but at the same time we are of direct noumenal origin. We belong to an Over-world of a higher order. We carry in the form and structure of our inner selves the mark and badge of linkage and kinship with a realm which can best be called Eternal, since it is real in its own essential being and of the same Nature as God who is the centre of its life and of ours.

Men in all ages, ever since there were men, have felt this Beyond within themselves. They have traveled out beyond the frontiers of the seen, and have lived in mutual correspondence with the More that is akin to themselves. Saints and prophets and supreme revealers of the race have interpreted for the others vividly and vitally the splendor of their unique insights and contacts. But first, last and all the time, religion has lived and flourished because man in his inner deeps is in mutual and reciprocal correspondence with eternal reality, and is in some measure the organ of it. We are religious beings because we partake or may partake of this higher Nature and share by our inmost form of being in a realm that is *eternally real*. At one apex point within ourselves we break through the world of change and process and *belong* to another Order which may become our fatherland and home. Religion at its best is the discovery of home and fatherland.

CHAPTER V

SOME ESTIMATES OF THE VALUE OF THE SOUL

A FAMOUS psychologist has recently written a widely read book entitled, *Modern Man in Search of a Soul.*[1] This book does not give the modern man much light on how or where he is to find a soul. It makes the fact quite evident on the contrary that the soul is as elusive, as mysterious, and as hard to "find" as God is. It takes the reader into the unknown regions of "depth psychology" and carries him back and forth along the frontiers of the "psychic hinterland." It gives him peeps down into the deep secret springs of life beyond the area which consciousness lights up with its half-lights. It tells him that there is "dirt and darkness and evil in this psychic hinterland," that the depth beneath the conscious area is a bottomless cellar full of spooks and ugly faces, waiting their chance to bolt up the stairs and grin at him. But nowhere is there any "soul" in sight which "he" can call "his," nor any central self that is in control of the "legion" of "spooks" and "ugly faces." There can, I think, be no more serious business on our hands today than this search for a soul.

[1] Jung, Dr. C. G., *Modern Man in Search of a Soul,* London and New York, 1933.

There have been two major assaults on the dignity and grandeur of the human soul, both of which are ancient in origin and both of which have had modern revivals of intensity. The first may be appropriately called the Augustinian assault and the second the scientific process of rationalization.

St. Augustine, Bishop of Hippo (354–430), did not originate the doctrine of "total depravity." It is present in inarticulate fashion in Tertullian and St. Cyprian and in other forerunners. It is to be found no doubt in an implicit stage in St. Paul. St. Augustine did not hold the doctrine consistently. It does not fit harmoniously with many of his loftiest experiences, or with the noblest passages which we love to quote. But Augustine was the first Christian Father to give this view of human life a basic formulation and to make it an essential feature of Christian dogma.

There were many diverse strands of thought from many diverse sources which this remarkable Carthaginian genius wove together into the solid doctrinal cable that was to hold the minds of men in the western world like adamant for more than twelve hundred years. The most familiar of the strands in St. Augustine's doctrinal cable was the epic story of "the Fall" told in the third chapter of *Genesis*. The story is part of an extensive Semitic tradition. It had been told again and again in earlier Babylonian epics before the writer of *Genesis* took it and gave it its profound significance for the birth of moral conscience in the life of the race. It is one of the deepest and most remarkable of all pictorial attempts to image forth the immemorial collision between the lower instinctive urges in man and the higher ideal tendencies which link him with a realm beyond himself, and the impossibility of recovering innocence when once it is lost. But the story is primitive and naïve. It conserves its unique greatness only so long as it keeps its imaginative suggestiveness and does not drop to a dull level of literalness. To turn it into dogma is to miss its true glory. The "forbidden fruit" in the story is *real* in the same sense that the apples of the Hesperides are *real* in the Greek epic of Hercules, or that the trees with healing leaves in the New Jerusalem are *real* trees. Unfortunately St. Augustine took the story in its factual meaning and read it as a realist account of an actual event.

Even more influential in his mind was the strand which he took from Plato's *Dialogues*. Plato was in the highest degree gifted with poetical genius. At the crucial moment in the unfolding of his interpretation of life and the universe he almost always introduces a myth or a parable which was intended to produce a poetic spell on the mind of the reader and to suggest a solution that could not be put in the cold dry words of dialectic. One of his most frequent myths or parables is that of "the fall." The soul in us, he seems to say, lived and moved originally in the heavens as a companion of the divine beings of the upper world. We traversed the heavens, driving our two winged horses of the soul, seeing the absolute realities of the universe, and sharing the life of the gods. Then there came a tragic *fall*. The soul failed to nourish its wings with the sight of truth, beauty and goodness, or perhaps one of the winged horses of the soul became unmanageable and we slipped and fell to this mundane level. Here the fallen soul became encased and imprisoned in a material body and had to live henceforth like a man chained in a cave, seeing only the shadows of things thrown on the wall of his cave. And yet, though damaged by the fall, we never quite lose the memory, the shadowy recollection, of those realities which we saw every day before we *fell*.

Here again St. Augustine took poetry for fact and read highly imaginative and suggestive literature as though it were the factual report of a traveler writing a log, or a notebook. Read in this literal fashion Plato through his myths became in the western world the main source of the doctrine of "the fall."

The vivid apocalyptic literature which flourished between the period of the Maccabees and the formation of the Christian Church was rich in suggestive material and in imaginative content about the war in heaven, the fall of the angels, and the havoc to the human race through the fall of Adam, with its entail of woe. *Fourth Ezra,* which is *Second Esdras* of the Apocrypha, is a notable source of the view that Adam was the seed of the harvest of woe for the human race. "A grain of evil seed was sown in the heart of Adam from the beginning," this book declares, "and how much fruit of ungodliness has it produced unto this time, and yet shall produce until the threshing floor come!" [2]

And even more emphatically in the seventh chapter of the same book Adam is blamed for all our troubles, as follows:

Better had it been that the earth had not produced Adam, or else, having once produced him, to have restrained him from sinning. For how does it profit us that in the present we must live in grief and after death look for punishment? O thou Adam, what hast thou done! For though it was thou that sinned, the fall was not thine alone, but ours also who are thy descendants! [3]

Here we have plainly enough a similar account of the position which is familiar to us in *Romans* and *First Corinthians*. *Second Baruch* traces our troubles and anguishes, disease and death as well as sensual passion and the begetting of children to Adam's sin, thus:

> *For when he transgressed*
> *Untimely deaths came into being:*
> *Grief was named,*
> *And anguish prepared:*
> *And pain was created,*
> *And trouble consummated:*

[2] IV Ezra, IV, 30.
[3] IV Ezra, VII, 118-119.

And disease began to be,
And the begetting of children was brought about,
And the passion of parents produced.[4]

There is, however, a passage in *Second Baruch* which claims that man's moral nature remains unimpaired; that each man shapes his own spiritual destiny:

For though Adam first sinned
And brought untimely death upon all,
Yet of those who were born from him
Each one of them has prepared for his own soul torment
*   to come,*
And again each one of them has chosen for himself glories
*   to come.*
Adam is, therefore, not the cause, save only of his own
*   soul,*
But each of us has been the Adam of his own soul.[5]

The influence of St. Paul's Epistles was without doubt a major contribution to St. Augustine's thought, though there is no systematic formulation of the doctrine of the fall or of man's depravity in his writings. He had no one fixed and consistent theory of man's spiritual estate. As a Jew, however, with rabbinical training, he never thought of questioning the accepted tradition of his people and he took for granted the fact that "in Adam all men sinned" and "in Adam we all died." But the moment one passes from the free and imaginative literary passages in St. Paul's Letters to the rigid doctrinal formulations of St. Augustine, one sees how

[4] II Baruch, LVI, 6.   [5] II Baruch, LIV, 15-19.

much would have to be *read back* into St. Paul from a later time to make him Augustinian. Between St. Augustine and St. Paul came the legal-minded Tertullian (150–220), who had already in his day by his vivid pictorial style, and his bald literalism, prepared the way for the full-fledged depravity doctrine of the Carthaginian Saint.

But we know that there was another major influence operative in the formulation of the famous doctrine. That was the influence of an extraordinary movement known in history as "Gnosticism." It drew its pictorial material from a multitude of sources, using all available sacred writings, especially Persian literature, Plato's *Timaeus,* the Old Testament, Egyptian mythology, and Apocalyptic books for its imaginative constructions. The movement in all its stages conceived of the soul as "fallen" from a high estate and as being exiled and imprisoned here in the lower world in *matter.* For all the Gnostic systems *matter* was considered to be evil. It was the antithesis of spirit; it was at the opposite of the realm of light. Gnosticism formulated in the sharpest way a complete dualism between spirit and material flesh, light and darkness, the yonder and the here. The pictorial narratives of the Gnostic writers contained vivid accounts of the fall and greatly expanded the body of tradition about the creation of man and woman, and what was involved for the human race in the original debacle.

For nine years of the formative period of his life

Augustine was associated with leaders of the sect of the Manicheans. This movement was a fusion of Gnostic ideas with Persian, Oriental, and Christian teaching. This movement gave Gnostic dualism an extreme form of expression and it pushed to the limit the prevailing hostility to *matter, flesh, body* as an evil principle. The imprisonment of the soul in a material body was a direct result of the fall. The propagation of children by a physical act instead of by a creative act of God seemed to them to be one of the most tragic effects of the fall. Unconsciously Augustine's thought was ineradicably colored by the profound pessimism of Manichean dualism.

His own sinful youth, his inability to break the evil habits which enslaved him and his long struggle with a divided will, a lower self, gave added color to his dark view of human nature. He came eventually to believe that the act of procreation was the original sin of Adam —the forbidden fruit—and that therefore every child is born of sin and in sin, and that the entire race is involved in the ruin and catastrophe which Adam's sinful act entailed. His depravity doctrine in its final form was pounded out on the anvil of a furious controversy with the British monk, Pelagius, who took an excessively optimistic view of human nature. For Pelagius every child is born in the condition of Adam before he fell, with divine possibilities of life, and as capable of choosing what is good as of choosing what is evil. This optimistic humanism seemed to Augustine the acme of heresy and in his fierce combat with the Pelagian errors he went all the way over into complete pessimism about man's estate. The tendency of human nature is wholly perverse. The dice are all loaded against any possible throw of goodness on the part of mere man. No "spiritual" quality belongs to us by our original nature. We begin life utterly bankrupt. We have no native capacity to choose the good. Everything which concerns man's salvation is superadded by divine grace and must be, if it comes, a supernatural gift from above.

This assault on the native capacity of the soul of man, which St. Augustine made, stripped away from human nature every shred and rag of "merit," of inherent worth. The human soul is thought of as spiritually sterile in its entire sphere and form. Salvation in every instance is a stupendous miracle. The very *faith* by which the individual soul accepts the proffered prevenient grace must be divinely bestowed upon it from beyond itself. And thus the complete depravity of man is the occasion for the supreme glory of the divine plan of salvation through Christ. Luther implicitly took over this Augustinian view of human nature, and Calvin and Knox took it over explicitly, and in expanded form, into their systems of thought.

The main current of the Reformation thus carried on unabated, sometimes even exaggerated, this pessimistic conception of man's soul, considered to be unfree, spiritually sterile and desperately *prone* to evil. This conception of man appeared within the Roman Catholic Church in the interesting movement known as Jansenism and in the noble piety of the Port Royal saints. It underlay, too, the extraordinary mystical intensity of seventeenth-century Quietism. There can be little question that the constant reiteration, in Calvinistic sermons and declarations of faith, of the inherent, ingrained wickedness of man powerfully tended to produce an "inferiority complex" in the youthful listeners, and led many persons to accept life at this estimate of valuation, with a deep depression of their hope and expectation. "It's a nasty dirty world," they said to themselves. "What's the use of trying to change such hopeless conditions?" No wonder that many persons in their despair of earth turned to apocalyptic hopes of a relief expedition from the sky to end the sorry scheme.

It is important to note that this view of human depravity does not rest for its support on actual experience. It is a theoretical construction. It is built on texts of scripture and on inherited metaphysics. We all find enough to disturb us and to give us profound intimations that all is not right within; when we come back to our own experience and when we make a serious diagnosis of our inner selves, we discover a good deal of waywardness and perversity. But we do not find ourselves "depraved." We are mixed, we are complicated, we show many signs of having low tendencies in us, but the ultimate reality in our nature is not all evil, and the deepest color in it is not black.

The great crisis in modern history, the World War and its dark aftermath, has once again enveloped the race in a thick veil of pessimism and despair. Out of the debacle of our idealism and our spiritual hopes there has broken forth a new wave of apocalyptic expectations, and there has come a *crisis theology,* which has revived in emphasized form the utter inability of man to *do anything* of himself to discover God, or to promote his own salvation, or to be an organ of spiritual values. In Barthian theology one sees man pictured at the *nadir* of his spiritual capacity. The wrecking of the world by man's insane folly in 1914–18 has vividly revived the memory of the wreck which Adam is supposed to have wrought with his forbidden fruit.

No other persistent assault upon the dignity of the soul can compare with this theological one except that made by the materialistic formulations of scientific thought. Such a materialistic formulation appeared first in the western world in Greece in the late fifth century, B.C. It came as a corollary to the theory of atoms. Democritus, who was a contemporary of Socrates, held the position that there is nothing in the universe that is not composed of physical atoms, except empty space. These atoms fall by a necessity of their nature and then, by collisions with one another as they fall, vortexes or swirls are formed, and thus collocations or masses of atoms are made by which everything in the universe comes into existence. Souls are made by atoms as certainly as are banks of earth, and the gods, if there are any gods, are nothing but "clumps" of atoms of a more nimble order. Perception is due to a stream of atoms from objects going in through pathways of the senses and hitting the atoms which make up the soul. This bald materialistic theory of the original school of atomists was adopted by the Roman poet Lucretius, who gave it wide circulation in very noble hexameters.

In that great breakdown of faith in Athens which came after the Peloponnesian War, and which we call the era of the Sophists, the basic scepticism of the time was very largely due to a depression in the estimation of the scope and value of the soul. Man was reduced to a swirl of atoms and a play of material forces with no inward creative power over a capricious destiny.

The Socratic movement, born in the midst of this depression, properly includes Socrates, Plato, Aristotle, and the Stoics. It turned the tide of western thought strongly against materialism, and submerged the atomic theory. This constructive movement gave Christianity a solid philosophical structure of thought which was strikingly adapted to its unique genius, and which furnished the Middle Ages with an authoritative philosophy and a metaphysics that were congenial with a spiritual interpretation of ultimate reality and of man's inner nature.

The revival of Science, however, in the sixteenth and seventeenth centuries was marked by a deep-seated revolt against the teleology of both Plato and Aristotle, and it pointed irresistibly in the direction of mechanistic explanations. Descartes (1596–1650) reduced the external world, including plants and animals, to masses of matter moving at varying velocities in an accurately describable mathematical order. There is nothing occupying space which cannot be mathematically described and explained. Descartes intended to exalt and glorify the soul. He gave it the status of a substance. He took it out of the realm of space-occupying things. It was given absolute uniqueness, with a capacity to think the infinite. But despite his best efforts, the soul in Descartes' system blurs off into unreality. It is nothing but a device for thinking thoughts. It is not the seat of our emotions. It does not originate acts. It has no connection or correlation with the world of things. It has no "at-homeness" here below. It may *reign* like a hereditary sovereign, but it does not *rule* over any outside realm. It never emerges out of its sheer abstractness. It is an inscrutable X. It is an *inside* that has no *outside*. It is a "grin with no face." Somebody sooner or later was bound to say of it, as a later scientist was to say of the God of Deism, "that hypothesis can be eliminated." Both David Hume and William

James—to mention only two revolters—impatiently eliminate this *soul-in-behind,* and take the thoughts themselves to be the thinkers.

Hume was merciless in following the implication of his logic. Finding only one source of human knowledge, namely sensations, he could discover no ground in experience for the knowledge of a permanent self, and he went on ruthlessly to the conclusion that our inner life is nothing but a stream of *sensations* and *ideas,* which are copies of sensations.

Sir Isaac Newton, the superb genius who gave the modern scientific system its most adequate mathematical formulation, was a scientist concerned only with the space-occupying world-masses of matter obeying unalterable universal laws. That world of matter for Newton was a vast mechanism as completely calculable as is the movement of a child's spinning top. This scientific theory came to be called "the Newtonian theory." It was applied in turn to each new field of conquest—astronomy, physics, geology, biology, physiology, and finally to psychology. As the mighty march of science proceeded, the sphere of the soul, the mind, the understanding, underwent severe shrinkage. For Locke it was a *tablet* on which the outside world recorded facts in terms of received experience. For most scientists the soul (variously named) was a passive spectator of the cosmic process which makes up the *real events* of the world. It is a humble eye that looks out on an immense cinematograph show which goes on without any contribution from the eye that beholds it.

Little by little the shrinkage became greater. The assault on the sphere of the soul became more deadly. In the hands of one group of scientists consciousness with all its implications was relegated to a humble position of being an odd secretion of the brain, comparable to the bile which the liver secretes. T. H. Huxley raised the question whether consciousness might not be an *epiphenomenon,* which would mean that it has no function. It opens and shuts no gates of action. It is a lone spectator in a distant tower. It *observes,* but it has no power over the course of events, even the events of the body. It holds no tiller. It steers no ship. One would suppose that this must be the lowest depression the soul could reach. Not so. There was more shrinkage still to come.

The Behaviorists, carrying existing biological formulations to their logical limits and working out the lead which William James gave in his famous essay, *Does Consciousness Exist?* buried the last relics of the poor old soul, which like the character in Balzac's *Peau de Chagrin,* had slowly been done to death by repeated shrinkages. Life comes to be thought of as nothing but *behavior of adaptation* and, in beings of our order, consciousness is a fleeting awareness of behavior-moments. These processes of shrinkage have in the main been carried out by biologists and psychologists who were profoundly ignorant of the constructive philosophy, which not only rebuilt the spiritual world that Hume had destroyed but also greatly enlarged the empire of man's spiritual domain. This contribution will concern us later on.

Dr. Sigmund Freud and the New Psychologists, while not being so excessively materialistic in their interpretations as behaviorism is, pushed the debacle of the soul to a new stage of calamity. The Behaviorists quietly informed us that we did not have any soul at all and that there never had been any such reality, while the Freudians give us back a dim inside world of a sort with a terrible subcellar to it with trap-doors, out of which emerge complexes, inheritance-factors, dreams, Œdipuses, Narcissuses, imps of darkness, sex-urges, which make one wish he had once more his "empty house," swept and renovated. What a strange house of the soul has Freud built!

It must be said in all fairness that Freud has brought healing to many distraught persons. He has developed a technique which is often effective for the discovery and elimination of complexes and repressions and other causes of dissociation and hysteria. He has many times found the key which has successfully unlocked a tightly closed life.

But it can be just as certainly said that his conception of human life is repulsive and distorted and that his account of man's *psyche,* both above and below the threshold of consciousness, is a Freudian construction, not *homo sapiens* as he truly and really is. Freud has lived so long in the atmosphere of abnormality and has handled so many pieces of the broken earthenware of life that he has lost his perspective for reality and sees life tinged with the colors of his own mind. He has done much in these last fifty years to demonstrate the immense significance of the subconscious, which he calls the "unconscious," but here again he has been warped by his own hasty theories of it and he has lived and worked quite unaware of the divine splendor and spiritual possibilities of that *psyche,* which in his clumsy way he has been trying to mend.

Meantime there has come, as might be expected from such widespread confusion of thought, a serious depression in the popular estimation of the *worth of the soul*. These other low estimations of the soul's worth which we have been reviewing were one and all theoretical. They were due to the logic of a theological or a scientific or a psychological system. This popular depression which confronts us in the world today is in the field of practical life rather than in the sphere of philosophical theory. Life for many persons has, without much arguing about it, dropped to a low level. Its eternal significance has faded out. The vision of an adequate goal has grown dim. Interior resources, like those of so many banks, have shrunk or dwindled away.

We are only too familiar with the reports of persons

who can see no meaning in life when their stocks or bonds decrease in value or when their tangible assets disappear, and who forthwith reach for a revolver, or leap from a high window and end the sorry show. That practical depression is much more serious than the theoretical ones were. These latter mental constructions were usually "discounted" when the time came to act. The words were strong but they did not always weigh very heavily in daily affairs. Hume and the others always smuggled in the words, "I," "me" and "mine," and treated them as real. The "fall" happened a long time ago. Perhaps the effect of its havoc was a bit over-rated. In any case a good many persons forgot the theological theories and managed to live very happily and quite free from the pessimism of depravity. Even less did the theoretical conclusions of science disturb the rank and file of the people. Most persons were in the condition of the old Maine farmer who suffered a stroke. He said, "They tell me that I have lost my mind, but I don't miss it any!"

In spite of the restraining theory and the declaration that nobody has a soul, the wayfaring man somehow found that he did not *miss* what he had always called his mind or his soul. Huck Finn said that he knew he had a conscience, because it took up more room than all the rest of his insides put together. No matter how loudly these theories thundered in the abstract, conscience and consciousness for the common man kept right on doing

business at the old stand. You may insist in a class-
room lecture, or in a book, that a human person is nothing but a curious bit of the earth's crust, "fantastically
carved," and that all one's processes, within as well as
without, are only molecular processes; but one powerful breath of genuine love, one stroke of death which
empties the house of all that was precious to the heart,
is enough to sweep the theory clear out of the field.

It is not so, however, with this *practical* depression
of the soul's value. That tinges life all the way through
to its core. It has its origin in a habitual way of life.
It is born of action. It is not a mere mind-constructed
theory. It can be eliminated only by a profound re-
organization and reconstruction of life from within.
When Jesus said that the sin against the Holy Ghost
could not be forgiven, he was speaking of *a condition
of life,* not of a specific act. It is possible to have such
a drop or sag of character that one's sense of right and
wrong becomes confused. One no longer recognizes
love or forgiveness when they are bestowed. It is like
the loss of sight which comes to the fishes in the Mam-
moth Cave. The vision drops away when it is no
longer used. The Pharisees said that Jesus' deeds of
love and grace were instigated by Beelzebub. That perverse judgment indicated that they had sunk so low in
moral perception that they could not recognize love
when it was before their eyes. It was that situation
which called forth the solemn words about the sin

against the Holy Ghost. It was a deep-seated, slowly formed moral habit or drop in spiritual perception, about which he was speaking.

Our depression in spiritual values is in one respect like that situation. It is not primarily due to a logical or metaphysical theory. It is due to a long-established habit of putting "things" above the inward qualities of life. Society has been putting the seal of its approval on *acquisitiveness*. That is man's specific trait. "Success" has been a magic word. *To arrive* has been more important than to discover how to be beautiful and good when the goal is reached. The prizes have been awarded to the "go-getter." Our educational methods have too often aimed toward utility-results, and they have failed to be concerned with character planning and the formation of ideals of life. Neither the home, nor the school, nor the church has been in these recent years a training place for the formation of spiritual insight, or for the discovery of intrinsic values of life. We have all dimly known that life is a fine art, but we have somehow assumed that it was a peculiar fine art that needed no preparation or guidance or practice for its attainment. The way back to the rediscovery of the worth and dignity of the soul will be slow and painful, but it is in no way less important than is the recovery from our financial depression.[6]

Meantime through all these centuries a submerged

[6] Later chapters will deal with this *rediscovery*.

stream from the Alpine headwaters of our Christian religion has gone on flowing and carrying deep under the theological formulations, the scientific constructions, and the recurrent slumps of faith, a wholly different assessment of man's spiritual worth. The dark and pessimistic conception of man's essential nature came from the alien tributaries to the central Christian stream, not from the original stream itself. No ingenuity of dialectic could ever succeed in deriving these theories of life out of Christ's account of man or from his testimony to the significance of the soul. This situation is one more evidence of the pitiful fact that the Christianity of history has drawn extremely superficially upon this headwater fountain source of our faith and has been profoundly colored by the tributaries to it. We should have had a very different Christianity —and we should have a different world now—if it had been built upon what Jesus thought of the divine possibilities of man instead of upon what St. Augustine in the fourth century thought of the Satanic actualities of human nature. It would have made a difference if instead of repeating endlessly the words, "We are miserable sinners and there is no health in us," we had always believed with George Fox that "there is something of God in every man."

Jesus' approach to men was always one of daring faith in man. He recognized, as every true "cure of souls" does, that lives become sadly warped and twisted by sins, by shams and insincerities, and that a powerful reconstruction and transformation must take place before there can be complete spiritual health. He had no shallow diagnosis for sin and he never expected any man to be made good by a spray of rose water.

But he did expect, as his greatest parables indicate, that when a person truly *comes to himself,* when in a lucid moment he gets down below his follies, his mistakes, his shams and his self-deceits, he will want to go back home to his Father where he belongs and find the inward joy of being a son. He seems everywhere to imply that man essentially "belongs" to God. The basic nature is spiritual, not carnal. The crucial process is coming to oneself. It is his method with diseased souls to bring them back to their deeper original sources of faith. The unwarped child, with his spontaneous faith and confidence in goodness, is the best illustration of that spirit which fits the Kingdom of God. It is impossible to suppose that he believed that the little child was a depraved limb of Satan. It is not easy to interpret his words, "Their angels do always behold the face of my Father," but these words at least mean that the unspoiled child and the eternal Father have something in common. The preciousness, the infinite worth, of the individual soul forms a luminous atmosphere everywhere in his Gospel. It is, I think, the most unique feature of his message about life. How he arrived at this insight is nowhere explained. How he reached such an estimate of the worth of life is never told. It is more wonderful than changing water to wine or than opening a blind man's eyes, but it is never listed among his miracles. His main contention with the Scribes and Pharisees was that they reduced life to rules and regulations, that they made it consist of doing "things that are required" for conformity, and that they turned life into a utilitarian scheme of adjustment, to get or to avoid certain results, here or hereafter.

For him life is a glorious adventure on its own account. One does not live to get some fixed and determined extraneous result—one lives to *live*. If anything gets in his way and threatens to balk the full attainment of *life,* the obstacle is to be ruthlessly eliminated even at the utmost cost. It may be a hand, a foot or an eye that hinders life. Let it then be hacked off or gouged out, so that nothing shall interfere with the full realization of life. I am convinced that Jesus had no ascetic attitude toward life. I cannot find that he had any theory that *matter* was evil. There appears to be in him no hostility as such to business occupation, or to property, or to home or to family. His caution to his followers was that they should allow nothing on earth—home, family, houses, lands—to rival their central aim, to *enter into life,* and to find its complete meaning in what he called the Kingdom of God. Every cable which holds the soul from going all the way out to sea with God must be cut at all costs. It is *life,* not things, that matters. Life does not consist of the things that one possesses. On the contrary, one may "own the whole world" and still "lose all that life means." The most "foolish" of all characters described in the New Testament is the man who had such an abundance of "goods" that he had to tear down his barns and store-houses and build new ones on a grander scale, but who in the midst of his swollen estate never once thought of the welfare of his soul. At the moment when his outward expansion had reached its pinnacle he found himself face to face with the supreme issue of life, and there he was with no inward resources to meet it. "Thou fool," came the echo across the spaces, "thou hast everything *except* the one thing that matters— thou hast no richness of life toward God."

That significant parable tells the whole story. That is Christ's estimate of the value of life. Other things *count,* no doubt. Houses and lands are "good" to own and to possess. But only one thing is *absolutely good* in the estimation of Jesus, and that is "to win life," to "possess one's *soul.*"

CHAPTER VI

WHERE DOES "OUGHT" COME FROM?

THOMAS HOBBES in the seventeenth century passed an ugly sentence on human life in his famous phrase: "The life of man (is) solitary, poor, nasty, brutish, and short." That is the judicial estimate, not of a theologian, but of a renowned philosopher. I suppose there have been individual persons of whose life it would be a realistic account. But only one of the adjectives is essentially true of man's life, as I know it. Life is beyond question *short*. It may be "poor." It is never quite "solitary." It ought not ever to be either "nasty" or "brutish." And it is just this sublime fact of "ought" and of "ought not" which haunts our lives and calls them from the low, the brutish, and the nasty, and that brings a signal glory to human life. "I will grant you," Emerson said once, "that life is mean, but how did we ever discover its meanness?" How did we come to see beyond the low and the mean?

One of the profoundest of all our problems of life is the question of the origin of that inward compulsion which we express by the word "ought" and the reason why we obey its call upon us, especially when it conflicts, as it often does, with elementary interests of

pleasure, or of survival. Dr. George W. Crile said in a
lecture in Philadelphia a few years ago that the frontal
lobes of man's brain are organs of strategy by which
he has been able to maintain his survival in the world
full of deadly enemies. But these frontal lobes are
vastly more than organs of strategy for purposes of
survival. They are organs of ideal vision of what ought
to be, and sometimes that vision makes survival quite
impossible.

> *Though love repine and reason chafe*
> *I heard a voice without reply:*
> *'Tis man's perdition to be safe*
> *When for the truth he* ought *to die.*

The answer to the problem of the ground and origin of
"ought" is by no means an easy one. It involves a study
of *taboos* and the heavy weight they have laid upon the
human spirit. It demands a complicated study of those
subtle impulsions and compulsions which come from
the social group in which every individual person is
embedded. There can be no such "solitary" person as
Hobbes supposes, no isolated person. Our noble word,
"obligation," means literally "tied-in." It expresses
what is "due" or "owed" to the group, into which the
individual unit is bound by invisible bonds. In the
primitive stages of life these obligations, born out of
the group life, have the unconscious drive of instincts
and they act powerfully as the flywheel of society.

But slowly there comes a transition in the life of man —amounting to a mutation—when the individual person passes over in some measure from outside coercion to inward compulsions, or at least some moral geniuses of the race make that transition. The moral genius does not go wholly beyond the pulls and influences of his social environment. They still remain an inalienable part of his being, but he has somehow discovered in the depths of his soul a feeling of obligation to an ideal society which ought to be, but is not yet. He acts in reference to a world order not yet born, and the vision of it holds him with a pull greater than that of his instincts, or his taboos, or his habits, or his tribal loyalties.

Bergson well says in this matter: "Look at it how you will, you must always come back to moral creators who see in their mind's eye a new social atmosphere, an environment in which life would be more worth living. I mean a society such that if men once tried it they would refuse to go back to the old state of things." [1]

When this new stage of life, this vision of an ideal society, comes into play, there comes with it the feeling of "ought," which has an aspect that cannot be traced to the push of the environment. When we have duly allowed for all the impacts and pressures of the social group there is an unexplored remainder. There is something here which does not come from the outside.

[1] Bergson, H., *Morality and Religion,* p. 71.

We can find this precious remainder only through a genuine appreciation and appraisal of the depth of man's inner life and the infinite worth of spiritual personality. The transition from *what is* to *what ought to be,* from outside coercion to inward compulsion, does not apparently come to all races, or to all persons, but when it does come it marks an epoch in spiritual development and it is one of the main miracles of man's higher life.

Socrates up to a certain point was obedient to the will of the state. He refused to run away and save himself from the decree of death which had been imposed upon him by its laws. But in all the higher matters of life which concerned his own soul he found his direction from within and was one of those moral geniuses who "cannot do otherwise" than obey their inward compulsions which seem to come to them out of the deeps of the soul or from beyond it. Socrates said to his judges: "I do nothing but go about among you persuading you all, both young and old, not to take account chiefly of your bodies or of your property, but first of all to care for the improvement of your soul, how that can be at its best." For him, then, there is no exchange value for a man's real *life,* and that real life is primarily a matter of inward depth.

Plato took over Socrates' lofty estimate of the value of life and pushed the investigation of its inward depth and its connections with a Beyond still farther than his master had gone. For Plato there is a type of life which is beyond all calculation of value, because it is a life in communion with eternity, where *goodness* is the supreme reality. "This," he says in the *Symposium*, "is the life above all others which a man should live, in the contemplation of absolute beauty, a beauty which if you once behold, you would see not to be of an exchange value with gold or fair garments or any other attractions. What if a man had eyes to see the true beauty, the divine beauty, I mean, pure and unalloyed, not clogged with the pollutions of mortality and all the colors and vanities of earthly life! In that communion, beholding beauty with the eye of his mind, a man will be enabled to bring forth not images and copies of beauty but true realities, and bringing forth and nourishing true virtue, he will become the friend of God and he will be immortal!"

Jesus was supremely a person who *saw* life in its absolute value. Its rewards for him were wholly intrinsic, and the path of obligation for him took its rise out of the deeps of his own personal life. "For this cause was I born and to this end came I into the world that I might bear witness to the truth." "Ought" means here at length, in that exalted saying before Pilate, the affirmation of a life dedicated to an ideal end, not to a beaten path made by the past. "My meat," he would say, "is to do the higher will that is revealed from above." We are not surprised, when we take the measure of the full significance of life as he saw it, that he should have concluded, as he did, that there is no exchange value possible for *life:* "What will a man give in exchange for his *life!*" Nothing! There can be no exchange!

It is, I am afraid, on the whole a somewhat rare achievement in the world for men like us to discover the absolute worth of personality and to live as though we knew that life is of a worth that has no exchange value. The biological approach to life gives no warrant for such a lofty estimate of it as that given above would imply. Nor again, can we climb to such a height of appraisal if we assume that the end and aim of life is nothing more than the acquisition of as many items of pleasure as possible during the period of human existence. The test of life either on the biological basis of it, or on the pleasure theory of it, is the survival test, which means its success in conjugating the verb, "to eat," and in collecting as many pleasure items as possible while we are in the process of conjugating it.

One main reason for the present-day depression of value in the estimation of life has been the widespread acceptance of life as merely a biological process. Are there not ominous hairs on our arms? Are there not the telltale relics in our structure, which plainly link us with low and ignoble forms of life? Are not many of our instincts and emotions ineradicable hints of a non-spiritual pedigree? What can we say that will relieve us of the stigma of having passed through the embryonic stages of gills and tail and other painful reminders? We used to be told that we were little lower than the angels, now we feel proud to be encouraged to believe that we are a bit higher than the extinct pterodactyls that flapped their membranous expansions with joy in the upper air of the Mesozoic Age.

We have been halting for three-quarters of a century between two opinions: Are we accidental by-products of the earth's crust, or are we sprung from a spiritual source? Is man an improved simian, escaped from the jungle though still partly in it, or is he, notwithstanding his biological pedigree, essentially a child of God? Are we to be read and interpreted wholly in terms of biological ancestry, or are we beings who can be understood only in the light of our connection with a supersensuous world of transcendent meaning?

Those questions cannot be settled altogether in biological classrooms or by studying the habits of orangoutangs in the zoo. Nor, it may just as truly be said, will that question be settled by dogmatic preachers and by pulpit assertions. In any event, however it is settled, the present depression of spiritual stock has been in large measure due to the suspicion that the question was finally going to be answered in terms of the first alternative. This suspicion has been played up to its maximum note by a number of popular writers of the moment, and it has become widely current. If you hear a statement often enough it is assumed that *it must be true.*

Meantime the pillar scientists, what William James would call the "folio edition" ones, have been proclaiming, not from housetops, but from their laboratories and observatories, that this universe cannot be explained in terms alone of matter and motion, nor adequately interpreted without reference to realities and values which are essentially spiritual, nor can life of our rank be reduced to functions and behavior.

We shall not, however, expect to get our directions in these supreme issues of life from the leaders of science. It is not their business to tell us what men live by. It is their major task to describe and explain observed facts and to show how these facts can be interpreted by universal laws of operation. What men like us *ought* to be and *ought* to do is not a problem that can be dealt with by methods of analysis or by exact description of facts. It involves another kind of insight and another type of wisdom. The kindling word which will stir our hearts for greater living will neither be in terms of dogma nor in terms of scientific formulation. It will come from persons who are themselves aflame because they have authentic tidings of eternal realities.

The fact that in a world like this there are beautiful things, things which are felt to be exactly the way they ought to be, involves a different approach than the

and emotions, urges and springs that spur to action. We also share conscious awareness that things are happening around us. The child, too, quickly exhibits this entire stock in trade. One overtopping characteristic which a person exhibits that a biological animal does not, is *self-consciousness*.

Self-consciousness is that strange power we possess of holding on to our own personal identity in the midst of the flux and process of knowing and pursuing. We turn in upon our hidden inner life and recognize it as our very own. A type of consciousness has emerged at this stage which we may properly call *spirit*. We somehow climb the ladder of this self-conscious spirit and overspan both the subject and object in one indivisible unity and know that we know. We do this by a swift, immediate and intuitive act, not by an inferential process. It remains forever a mystery how it can be done, and yet it is the surest of all our facts of human experience.

When this power came to birth something unique came to pass, though there may have been dim prophecies of it in the higher forms of life. Mind in beings like us has to a degree now detached itself from its dependence on objects in space. It has become spirit and can attend to a spiritual object of its own order. Mind as spirit has succeeded in emancipating itself from identification with body, with the things that are perceived by senses. It can see with its inward eye—can, in fact, behold itself as an object. There is nothing else like that power, that capacity, to be found anywhere in the world.

It is through the unity of a perduring self, of the type which self-consciousness reveals, that *knowledge,* as distinguished from mere awareness, becomes possible. If we could not grasp a new fact of mental experience and weave it into the fabric of our past experience and appraise its meaning in relationship to that past experience, felt to be our own experience, we could never say, "I *know.*" It involves an overspanning type of mind, such as among all the beings we know only man possesses. It is a type of mind that can hold its own identity while it binds many items of perception, memory and imagination into one living whole, with the added consciousness, "*I* know it and I know that it *must* be so." This unique self-consciousness is the citadel of our sanity as persons. It is the mental mill through which all the scattered items of sensation are drawn into a central unity of knowledge and marked with our peculiar brand of ownership, somewhat as our overspanning minds get the single symphony out of the music of a multitude of diverse instruments. It is the solid basis of all that we are, of all that we know, and of all that we hope for.

We also have, we alone among all biological beings, the unique power of developing ourselves by the lift of ideal forecasts. We only can say with Edmund Burke:

"We are in great degree the creatures of our own making." I am not now thinking of the so-called "self-made" men, who may or may not have completely finished their creations! I am thinking of that marvelous power which we all as persons possess of looking before and after and of blazing forward a new trail of life out of the blended experience of memory and imagination. *We* have the novel capacity of living by forward pulls and not alone by causal pushes from behind. For us the gates of the future are open. The future is as much a fact and counts with us as much as the past does. Anticipation plays as great a rôle in our drama of life as the actors of memory do. Our goal is always a flying goal and in all our intelligent fore-reaches it is a new and more inclusive self that we as creative artists are fashioning. Oliver Wendell Holmes got his fine illustration from a humble animal of the sea, but only a person of the poet's type could have said to himself:

> *Build thee more stately mansions, O my soul,*
> *As the swift seasons roll!*
> *Leave thy low-vaulted past!*
> *Let each new temple, nobler than the last,*
> *Shut thee from heaven with a dome more vast.*

This power in us to look before and after and to build our lives by the lift of ideal forecasts which have a forward pull involves another unique trait. Only self-conscious persons who are free spirits like us can span

time and bind it into a living unity. We alone can recover a past time that was dead and can make it alive
again in a living present, and at the same time can
know that the recovered past was our past and that the
living present holds in one span of unity both past and
present. This capacity to rise above time and overspan
it gives us an intimation of eternity in the midst of time.
Eternity is the experience of holding and possessing in
one moment the here and now, the past and present
and that which is to come. Out of that unique duration-
span which we feel going on in the stream of our own
life, we are able to create by forecast a new event quite
unlike what would have happened without the revival
of the past in the living pulse of the present, which was
at the same time big with a momentous future.

This time-transcending power is very much in evidence in the enjoyment of music. Here the musical
notes are not passively received by the mind as a
seriatim succession, like a row of dots. The mind of the
music-lover rises above the temporal sequence of the
notes and holds them together in an inclusive time-
span which forms a harmonious whole. Mozart in a
famous passage which I quote only in part has vividly
described this experience. "I do not, as I compose,
hear the notes one after another, as they are hereafter
to be played, but it is as if in my fancy they were *all at
once*. While I am inventing, it all seems to me like a
vivid dream; but hearing the piece all at once, that is

the best experience. What I have heard in that way once I never forget, and perhaps this is the best gift God has granted me."

Not less important, and assuredly not less unique, is the power which we as persons apparently possess of self-direction. Tennyson rightly calls it man's main miracle:

> *This main miracle, that thou art thou,*
> *With power on thine own act and on the world.*

I am not interested for the moment in the abstract problem of free-will, which in the end always gets its answer from one's ultimate theory of the universe. I want to focus attention rather upon what our own personal self-conscious life reveals—in short, on what it means to be a person. When we turn away from dogmatic theories and come to the testimony of our own consciousness, nothing seems more obvious than that our minds are selective, or that there is direction from within. Our kind of consciousness is essentially dynamic; it opens and shuts doors of action. The only reason for doubting such a spontaneous capacity, a capacity which we all feel in our moments of high decision, is the fundamental doubt, which some persons have, that anything "spiritual" can be real.

This spontaneous release of the energy of spirit, if it be granted, would mean that there is a possibility in us, or at least in some of us, of going beyond ourselves on occasion and of *becoming more than we ever were before.* It would mean that some persons, at crises in their lives, may transmit a power of life quite beyond anything that they have received from any traceable sources. Paradoxical as it seems, more may come forth than has ever been put in. We as persons are within limits *creative.* We have not dealt with the full scope of the life of a person unless we have felt this amazing *possibility* of spontaneity. I am well aware that that possibility will not be granted by all of my hearers or readers. Many of us are so accustomed to the method of equations—the future being equal to the sum of the factors of the past—that we shall not easily accept an event which can be traced to no adequate antecedents except the inward spirit itself.

It seems to me that *transcendence* belongs inherently to the full meaning of a personal spirit. The complete nature of a person could never be *found* by adding the sum of its past experiences, nor could its next stage of experience ever be predicted by summations of the past. There is always a *beyond* which cannot quite be accounted for in terms of calculation. We can never say, "I am." There is "more" which must be waited for. "We partly are and wholly hope to be." It is impossible to make *immanence* intelligible without *transcendence,* even in the case of our own personal spirits.

We must finally consider the person as a carrier of

intrinsic values. Equation values are very familiar to us and present no mystery. It is considered in every way rational to *give* in order to *get*. Everybody understands a *quid pro quo*. Commercial and economic values are of that order. But intrinsic values are of a different order; they are unique; they cannot be explained biologically; they exist only for persons who can rise above "calculation" and feel the immediate worth of something for its own sake. We enjoy beauty without any reinforcement from beyond itself. We face duty and obey the call of *ought* out of pure loyalty to our vision that this new deed *ought to be*. We love, when we are at our best and noblest spiritual stature, not for utilitarian reasons, or because we hope to get an equation in return, but because we have found a beloved object which calls out our utter devotion without any calculations of what may come back to us. Not all experiences of beauty, or of duty, or of love, by any means, are as intrinsic and pure as that account would indicate. The creator of beauty often thinks of his work of art as a commodity. The moral reformer who takes the difficult and sometimes dangerous path of duty may very well have mixed motives in his mind. The state of mind which I have been calling "ought," is not necessarily one hundred per cent pure *categorical imperative*. Even in the overwhelming feeling, "I cannot do otherwise," there may be a fringe of selfish color. Nor, again, is love—even love for truth—always refined and sublimated to such a point that it is utterly devoid of self-seeking features.

All that we can say is that there are, at least on rare occasions, exalted values of life which cannot be reduced to extrinsic or utilitarian calculations, nor explained on a basis of desire for any kind of returns. We do not live by bread and butter alone. We cannot be subsumed under biological categories. We do not easily fit into a system of equations. As self-transcendent persons we introduce a new order of standards and estimates. Beings who *obey an ought* belong in a unique class and cannot be interpreted completely in terms of lower forms of life, or of what was here before this unique trait emerged.

The issue turns, or at least seems to me to turn, on the possession of a capacity of *transcendence*. Things in general, and beings below our level, are bound to keep to fixed limits. Their place, their movement, and their goal are in a high degree predictable. It probably is not quite true of any scale of life, but we know well enough and near enough what an amoeba will do next and what the reactions of a chimpanzee will be under given circumstances. The lines are in the main fixed and the grooves are rigid. They are what they are, and "that's the end on't." No doors of surprise open outward or upward from within them. They cannot roll up the past and create a novel event.

The advance, well-nigh infinite, which we as persons

have made over our predecessors is, that somewhere within a door has been flung ajar—a magic casement—which opens on unexplored worlds of a higher order. We have intimations of wider scope. We have appetites which no fruits of trees on earth will satisfy. We live out beyond ourselves and somehow eternity has got into our hearts. We are not set in rigid finite limits; we are finite-infinite, with "a more yet," beyond every attainment.

It is, I claim, because we belong to this Over-world of a spiritual order that we have intimations of *what ought to be.* We see beyond what is. We are more than the summation of the past. The gates of life open for us on possibilities that are not yet made actual. We see the path of spiritual advance not by our senses but by the creative power of our minds which are akin to this Over-world of higher reality.

When we ask why we *obey* our vision of ought, the answer is easy. When once we truly *see* what ought to be and feel its compulsion it eliminates alternatives from our mind. We say, "how otherwise." What ought to be simply *ought to be.* The whole problem is the problem of *seeing* it. There is no arguing about beauty and in the same way there is no arguing about *ought* when it clearly breaks in on the soul. Emerson is nobly right when he speaks in the lines I have already quoted of hearing a voice "without reply." Our difficulties come, of course, from the fact that we are amphibians and live in two realms. We *are* biological. We do live up to a point by bread. We have utilitarian interests. We are creatures with urges and drives and instincts. They often conflict with ideal visions which link up with our other World. We must choose which world is our real fatherland. But the burst of a great love when it really comes, sweeps away all doubts and wherefores. So here, too, when we find the true fatherland of the soul we recognize its call and we answer, "Here am I."

Anker Larsen, the distinguished Danish novelist, is the author of a remarkable little autobiographical book, entitled, *With the Door Open*. He has discovered the difference between the lower and the higher world. He calls it the difference between "asthmatic gasping" for breath and having a current of fresh air rush into the lungs. It is the difference between everyday interests and radiant ecstasies of the newness of life. Larsen says that the experience feels like the actual meeting of the soul with Eternity. The person who has it, he says, feels purified and healed as though he were animated by God's own breath.

If these unique traits and possibilities belong to the nature of a person then such a person possesses what may be rightly called *infinite worth*. There is no assignable exchange value for a life like that. There is nothing finite for which it should be bartered. This was always and everywhere Christ's estimate of the precious-

ness of the human soul. It is an insight which is easily
lost and which is always recovered with difficulty. The
Augustinian view of human nature and of its inherent
corruption has often eclipsed the original Christian
view of man's unique endowment.

George Fox, a contemporary of Thomas Hobbes,
went about proclaiming that there is something of God
in man. Out of one of his most intolerable prisons he
sent a message to his followers, urging them to "walk
cheerfully over the earth answering that of God in every
man." He proposed to treat every man and woman and
child as infinitely precious. It remained for Immanuel
Kant, by the methods of his critical philosophy, to es-
tablish more clearly than any other modern thinker had
done the fact that we as persons possess a capacity of
Reason through which *we can determine our lives by
the idea of what ought to be*. For him the will toward
the good in a person holds the supremacy over everything else in nature. "The only thing in this world, or
in any possible world that is *good* without qualification,
is a good will."

The morally good will stands, for Kant, as the cen-
trally creative thing in the life of a rational person, and
for him it exalts the person to an infinite worth. It
was in the light of that supremacy that Kant finally
formulated his categorical imperative in these words:
"So act as always to treat humanity, whether in thine
own person or in the person of another, as an end, never

as a means." Tennyson, as those know who are familiar
with his life, was deeply under the influence of Kant's
philosophy, and frequently in *In Memoriam* translated
Kant's noblest ideas into noble poetry in many of the
stanzas of that poem. The original poem closed with a
remarkable interpretation of the supremacy of the good
will.

> *O living will that shalt endure*
> *   When all that seems shall suffer shock,*
> *   Rise in the spiritual rock,*
> *Flow through our deeds and make them pure,*
>
> *That we may lift from out of dust*
> *   A voice as unto Him that hears,*
> *   A cry above the conquered years*
> *To one that with us works, and trust,*
>
> *With faith that comes of self-control,*
> *   The truths that never can be proved*
> *   Until we close with all we loved,*
> *And all we flow from, soul in soul.*

Chapter VII

RELIGION: A MUTUAL AND RECIPROCAL CORRESPONDENCE BETWEEN GOD AND MAN

It was Clement of Alexandria at the end of the second century who used this striking phrase, "mutual and reciprocal correspondence." Correspondence means to us, no doubt, something quite different from what it could have meant for Clement in his remote century. The Victorians of the last generation taught us the phrase, "Life is correspondence with environment." To live, for them, was to correspond with environment. Failure to "correspond" meant death. There are certain things, like oxygen and food, in the external environment which are essential to physical life, and when the individual, trapped in a mine, for instance, fails to make contact with either food or oxygen, he dies from his failure of correspondence. Among the myriad forms of life that swarm over the earth, each individual type possesses some peculiar organs and aptitudes for making the essential correspondence. Some types live where other types cannot survive, because the former are gifted with methods of correspondence which the latter lack. Some forms of life exhibit remarkable *tropisms,* or tendencies to turn toward the sources of life in their environment. They live because they push out their tiny rootlets or their slender tendrils in the direction of supplies to live by. They survive because they successfully correspond.

It is quite possible that this conception of life as correspondence with environment may furnish us with a fresh suggestion for considering the essential nature of religion. Religion in its deepest significance may turn out to be mutual and reciprocal correspondence between the soul and its invisible environment. In that case, to live spiritually would be to correspond with the essential environment of the soul. Ernst Troeltsch in recent times used quite similar language to that of Clement. He held that revelation is not a simple, one-sided effect of God's activity on man's soul. It is a reciprocal process. "The human and the divine," he declared, "co-exist in a complex *mutual interpenetration.*" [1]

Plotinus, who lived in Alexandria the next generation after Clement and who was a fellow-student with Clement's famous pupil, Origen, held the view that man is an amphibious being, since he can live in either one of two worlds. He can live out toward the periphery of his world and "correspond" with things in space and

[1] Troeltsch's "Theory of Religious Knowledge." In *American Journal of Theology,* Vol. XXIII, p. 279.

time that are similar in nature to his body, or he can live up toward the divine centre of being and "correspond" with those eternal realities which are adapted to the higher nature of his soul. No person can travel so far outward toward the material fringes that he will not at times feel a tug upon his soul which pulls him back toward the "dear fatherland," where he really "belongs." There are, then, Plotinus holds, these two levels of life open to all of us. Each level of life has its peculiar environment and we, as great amphibians, can "correspond" with either the one or the other as we will—we can live upward or we can live downward and outward away from the trails that lead toward the true home of the soul. As Richard Watson Dixon has expressed it:

> There is a Soul above the soul of each
> A mightier Soul which yet to each belongs.

St. Augustine, who in his early period was profoundly influenced by the writings of Plotinus, and who more than once wrote passages which are reminiscent of passages in this great forerunner, explained our human restlessness by the fact that we "belong" to a higher order of life, and are so made that we can rest only in correspondence with that Life above us to which we belong—"Our hearts, O God, are restless until they find rest in Thee."

There is a vivid and impressive story in the Book of

Kings which tells how a young prince named Hadad of the royal family of Edom, fled from Edom to escape Joab, David's captain, who had vowed to kill every male person in that country. Hadad reached Egypt in safety, was taken into Pharaoh's palace, grew up in his household and finally married the sister of Pharaoh's queen, who bore him a son. Years went by, Hadad prospered, became as one of the princes of Egypt, lived in plenty and luxury, but when he heard that David was dead and that his old enemy Joab had gone to his reckoning, Hadad came to Pharaoh and asked that he might depart and go back to his own country. "Why!" Pharaoh answered in surprise, "what hast thou lacked here in Egypt with me that thou seekest thine own country?" "Nothing," replied Hadad, "howbeit, let me go to my own country!" That "howbeit" reveals the mysterious pull of the true fatherland and sweeps away all arguments of expediency.

This story was not written as a parable or allegory, but there could be no better illustration of the migratory longing of the homesick soul for its fatherland, its country of birth.

> *Hence in a season of calm weather*
> *Though inland far we be,*

there is an unmistakable upward pull on the soul, which makes all the allurements of the world of time and space and things seem poor and thin in comparison with the attraction of the world to which we really "belong." "Howbeit let me go to mine own country!"

We must not, however, hastily assume that this haunting nostalgia, this homesickness of the soul, means an eagerness to die and go to a peaceful heaven beyond the stars. Not that. It means rather the discovery that here in the midst of our busy life in this domain where the body is at home, we have an ampler environment in which our entire being can expand and live. It is not to some other "place" that we want to go. It is rather to another amphibian level or dimension in this strange double-storied world in which we find ourselves.

Religion of the true creative quality comes to birth in us and becomes a power to live by when the soul awakes to the real presence of its actual environment, which was always there, and begins to "correspond" with it vitally. One of St. Paul's greatest sayings is the promise that when life attains to its fullness, "We shall know even as all along we have been known" (I Cor. XIII:12). This passage is not a solitary reference to such mutual intercourse. It is a frequent thought with St. Paul that spiritual relationship is divine-human interrelationship. That means, I think, that the correspondence which in our unawakened stage has been one-sided, i.e., from above down, will become "mutual and reciprocal." The soul when it becomes *aware* will find its real environment and will rise to its true life by corresponding with that environment.

One of the greatest weaknesses of much that passes for religion is its abstract and bloodless quality. God is thought of as a logical concept. He is up at the end of a ladder of arguments. He is a Being about whom men speculate and debate. He is sought as the conclusion of a syllogism, or at the top of a high Babel-tower constructed of proof-texts, or He is affirmed in an ancient creed which we learned once. But not thus does He become a warm and intimate Person whose reality makes our hearts tingle, and who sends us forth with thrill and enthusiasm for high adventure and infinite hazard. We do not sell all we possess for such pearls. We are only too familiar with this cooled and slowed-down "faith." All too frequently congealed notions "about" these great matters are presented to the passive minds of listeners, but not thus does the water change to wine and not thus the dead are raised to life. We need to emerge out of that stage of arrested development in religion, this scheme of abstractions, and have the miracle of the day-dawn and the day-star in our hearts.

Significant religion from the earliest childhood of the race until this moment in history is always and everywhere mutual and reciprocal correspondence. It is man's discovery of an *Other than himself* who is all the time in correspondence with him, and from whom comes health and healing. Isaac Penington in the joy of such an experience said: "This is He, there is no other. I have felt the healings drop into my soul from under His wings." God does not begin in our consciousness as *an abstract Idea:* He is first of all a real presence, not an inference. He is an experience, the Ground and Basis of all our other knowledge and of all the values which attract us. The reality of God is directly "borne in upon us" as an experience, to use Charles Bennett's phrase, before we make our philosophical inferences of His existence. Our proofs of God, as he suggests, are ways of reminding ourselves of what we have already discovered. We are *religious* because as human beings we are indivisibly related to a World of the spiritual order. We are *religious* because as rational beings we are bound to transcend ourselves through intercommunication. We cannot live as mere finite spirit. We are bound to correspond with the environment on which our life depends. I am convinced that religion in the child, and in the race, takes its rise from awareness of an Other, who is both within and beyond the world that is seen, and within and beyond the mind of the beholder.

Anker Larsen, in the book already mentioned, *With the Door Open,* has happily told of the peace and repose that come to the little child when the "direct unconcealed smile of eternity" rests upon him. "Who has not been moved," he asks, "at the sight of a small boy standing silently absorbed in himself, with the halo of innocence on his head? The small boy is not in any way in need of our help; he stands perhaps in the middle of his father's farmyard, and from the window his mother's eyes are watching over him. But he stands at the same time in the midst of the Eternal and reminds us of the Paradise we have lost." [2]

No one has more vividly described the child's joy and wonder than has Thomas Traherne. "Adam in Paradise," he wrote, "had not more sweet and glorious apprehensions of the world than I had when I was a child. All appeared new and strange at first, inexpressibly rare and delightful and beautiful. I was a little stranger, which at my entrance into the world was saluted and surrounded with innumerable joys. My knowledge was divine. I knew by intuition those things which since my Apostacy I have collected again by the highest reason. . . . Eternity was manifest in the Light of Day, and something infinite behind everything appeared: which talked with my expectation and moved my desire. The city seemed to stand in Eden, or to be built in heaven." [3]

A recent Welsh writer of much insight, Rees Griffiths, has taken the consistent position that self-consciousness implies a God-consciousness, that is, an awareness of an Other Mind who is the All Knower, and the intelligent Unity of Knowledge. For this writer the sense of God is prior to and conditions the sense of

[2] J. Anker Larsen: *With the Door Open,* p. 79. Macmillan.
[3] *Centuries of Meditation,* pp. 156–158. London: Bertram Dobell.

duty, so that instead of making morality condition religion, as Kant did and many others do, he would treat religion as the social atmosphere within which all moral action and thought and feeling must develop.[4] God becomes thus the spiritual environment of our souls, out of which all the higher processes of life germinate and blossom.

The doctrine of "emergence" in evolution is so far only a theory. It is still in the stage of hypothesis, but if it ever comes to be a generally accepted method of explaining evolution, we shall trace the new and previously unpredictable forms that "emerge," not to some vague and unsuspected potentiality in matter, but to the creative influence of an environing Mind which broods not only over the birth-processes of finite spirits like us, but as well over the significant mutations which mark the crisis through which the cosmos moves forward on its slow upward way toward the completer world that is to be and that is already coming to be. We shall not always be led astray by "the genetic fallacy," by which so many persons today gaily assume that higher forms of life are only complicated aggregations of lower forms, and that the unique aspects which have emerged are to be read and interpreted only in terms of a lowly origin.

My primary interest now, however, is not in speculative theories of emergence, but in the deeper meaning

[4] See Rees Griffith's *God in Idea and Experience,* p. 250.

of our own human experience. I want to point out how self-consciousness in its higher aspects reveals the presence of an Other Mind, a creative environment in which we all live and move and have our essential being. "We cannot genuinely conceive ourselves," Professor W. E. Hocking well says, "as mentally alone in this cosmos.". . ."My dependence upon Nature," he continues, "my momentary submission to its independent, obstinate, objective decision of what Fact and Truth shall be, both in principle and detail—is not this a finding of my own mind? It is here in this momentary (as well as permanent) creation of my Self that I begin to find Nature taking on the aspect of an Other Mind." [5] In a recent article, Dr. Hocking has even more emphatically asserted that God is "an experience of my Other Self, inalienably present." "As I find myself," he says, "so I find therewith an immediate sense of God." [6]

There is a native mysticism operating in the mind of the child as he discovers the reality of his world and the reality of other minds and the trustworthiness of his own experience. It is odd that the child, with possible rare exceptions like that of Wordsworth, does not feel as though the world around him were the *projection* of his own mind. "Solipsism" is a philosophical theory of later life, not a discovery that comes to trouble a

[5] *God in Human Experience,* pp. 278–287.
[6] *Christian Century,* March 8, 1933.

child. What he sees and hears and touches is from the first *real* for him, real in form and order, and there just as it looks. The "ego-centric predicament" is not a disease of childhood, it is a highly sophisticated problem which troubles only minds "debauched" by much reflection. The child at the beginning "knows as he is known." The ordered world of stable reality comes to him as though there were an Other Mind conversing with him, and he trusts it with an implicit faith. The world out there is not felt to be the "creation" of the child's own mind. It is "found" ready-made and is "accepted" in all its stubborn *otherness,* and as soon as the child grows conscious in his dim twilight of a self, he is in the same moment conscious, also in dim twilight, of a More than himself as the Other Mind that is involved in the nature of the world, which he is discovering and which contributes to him.

At length the man who has traveled farther from the East and who has graduated from mysticism into cold and sharply defined logic, still finds his world crammed with meaning which is even more stubbornly *other* than it was in childhood. It is penetrated from husk to core with law and order. It moves from microscopic atom to telescopic nebula with mathematical regularity. It is correlated at every point with his own intelligence, but strangely enough he fails now to get clear hints of an Other Mind. It is more than probable that if a full account were taken by this logical person of all that is involved in the nature of self-consciousness and of all that is bound up with the knowledge of truth as *truth,* he might still discover that this child mysticism, which implicitly finds an Other Mind, is genuine wisdom and is well on the way to reality.

Knowledge of truth, that is to say, knowledge when it reaches beyond momentary and particular sense experiences, and *apprehends reality,* implies a much wider range of spiritual life than that of a mere finite knower. To know that a truth is universally, necessarily and eternally true presupposes much more than my temporary state of mind and more than anything that my solitary mind could ever attain. When I announce that I *know* I am appealing from my solitary self to One that is a larger inclusive Mind and that binds coherently together both me as the knower and the object that I know, in an indivisible whole. "I know as I am known." We cannot genuinely believe in ourselves and in our precious truth without at least implicitly believing in the God in whom we live and through whom we know the truth. But so far we have been concerned with what is *implied* in thought, not with what is consciously *experienced.*

When we pass from the implications that are involved in self-consciousness to the actual awareness of an environing Mind, as the child does, and as many others do who have traveled far inland away from the coasts of childhood, we have religion as it is in its essential meaning. In the early dawn of self-consciousness when expectation is high, it is easy to pass from *implication* to *awareness*. As Browning puts it in *Bishop Blougram's Apology:*

> *Time and earth case-harden us to live;*
> *The feeblest sense is trusted most; the child*
> *Feels God a moment, ichors o'er the place,*
> *Plays on and grows to be a man like us.*

But fortunately we do not all "scar over" the sensitive place in us where we make our contacts with Eternity. Some of us "become like little children" even after we have enriched our minds with the accumulated wisdom of the world, and we discover that lost smile of eternity.

There is a well-known prayer in the *Prayer Book* which asks "that we may so pass through things temporal that we finally lose not the things eternal." That word "finally" in the prayer has an ominous significance. It means that we must not expect to find eternal realities here in this "vale of mutability," but *finally* "after life's fitful fever is over," and we have entered the domains of peace we shall, if we are fortunate, have the joy of eternity! Now that word "finally" was not in the prayer as it was originally written. The writer of the prayer in its noble intention was asking that we might so pass through things temporal that even in the midst of these things of time we shall not lose the consciousness of eternity. *That* is a great prayer in every way worth praying. But so many persons in this busy and material world lose their joy and wonder, and suffer a depression of expectation, that "finally" becomes a natural measure of their hope. They postpone the rosy dawns of eternity to the great tomorrow when "time shall be no more." For them eternity comes after time, not in it, and through it and around it. Shakespeare with his usual depth of wisdom speaks in *Macbeth* of "this bank and shoal of time." It is for him a little island in the midst of eternity, like St. Helena in the immense sea that pours around it. Eternity invades time at many points. There are many hints of mutual and reciprocal correspondences. The invisible impinges on the visible and the one has emerged out of the other, and the visible depends upon the invisible for its being.

A few summers ago a gentleman spending his holiday on the coast of Maine volunteered to teach a Sunday School for the native children who lived on a tiny island of the region. He went out in his motor boat on the first day of his experiment and gathered the children about him to begin the lesson. He thought he would start with what they all knew and proceed from that to what would be less well known. With an encouraging smile he asked, "How many of you have seen the Atlantic Ocean? All that have seen it, raise your hands." Not a single hand went up. They had never heard before that it was the Atlantic Ocean. They could see it from every part of the island; they heard it roar as they went to sleep, and they listened to its beat upon the shingle of the shore when they awoke in the morning. All their ventures were on its waters. They swam in it, they went out in boats on its surface, they caught fish from its deeps. But they thought it was just ordinary water. Of the world-wide sweep of the Atlantic Ocean, of that they knew nothing, not even its name.

It may stand as a simple parable of the lives of many persons who are encamped upon "this bank and shoal of time." They could not live a breath without the greater world around them. They could not know the simplest *truth* without a *more than themselves*. They could not *be* at all without a Beyond akin to themselves, and yet they stare out upon the surrounding Sea which makes their tiny island possible, without knowing the name of it and without awakening to the environment which is essential to their life and thought. Our universe in its totality must be vastly greater and richer than our senses report. Once no one suspected the invisible world of atoms and plasms, of radiations and vibrations, which we have discovered. Our visible world has plainly come out of an invisible world upon which it rests, and it could not last an hour without the invisible realm to complete and maintain it. Just as certainly there must be an environment of another order which sustains the soul and completes its destiny.

The moral life of man is one of the supreme evidences of this mutual and reciprocal correspondence. Dr. Nicolai Hartmann, in his monumental work on *Ethics,* takes the ground that "Conscience is the influence upon us of a higher Power. It is a Voice from another world—the world of ideal values." [7] He continues, "It speaks out of the depth of one's own being, uninvited, unexpected, mysterious, and it speaks authoritatively and convincingly." "It is," he concludes, "the primal consciousness of value which is found in the feeling of every person."

Conscience is unmistakably something more than our own wish, or will or insight. It is the influence upon us of some reality beyond ourselves that produces in us the august sense of *ought.* A being that lived only in itself and revealed no self-transcendence would have no more ground to be considered "moral" than would any "crop-full bird" or "maw-crammed beast." Until ideals come to birth there is no "ought." But at the same time I feel sure that it is a mistake to imply that our conscience is a Voice from another world, or a "mechanism" in us for reporting moral decisions arrived at by another Will than our own. There can be no morality for us if we are not self-legislative persons with our own area of freedom and our own autonomy. We are not puppets acting as we are pulled and pushed. We are arbiters of our own destiny. We are selective agents in our own right and we determine our own

[7] *Ethics,* Vol. I, p. 201.

moral deeds. This majestic business of life, however, is possible for us because self-consciousness opens out into God-consciousness, because we are ourselves plus a More. We live out beyond the boundaries of our finite selves. We open within upon a world where ideals are real and where the *good* of which we catch glimpses has eternal being. We constantly form ideals of a goodness which goes beyond what we have so far found "existent" in the structure of our time-world, just as we constantly find beauty out there in the world where science can give us no basis for it.

Neither beauty nor goodness can be explained in terms of masses of matter moving at calculable velocities. They both, as intrinsic values, testify to another world than the one we weigh and measure or where we add and subtract. It is often assumed that we find God because we are inherently moral. The moral will is thought of as the gate to the spiritual world. I believe the reverse is the true order. We are conscious of duty, we feel obligation, we pursue ideals, we are the builders of kingdoms of the spirit because we have already found God, and have discovered "the magic casement" which opens into His realm of life. The correspondence has all the time been mutual. The words, "Behold, I stand at the door and knock," mean more than at first appears. They present the whole story of the deeper world knocking at the doors of earth. It is an announcement of the eternal coming of God to men.

But it is never a one-way process. It is forever a double search. Hands of prayer have been raised ever since there were men. The foolish builders of Babel on the Plains of Shinar do not exhibit the only way there is of climbing up to the place where God is. Wherever love is, there God is. Wherever beauty draws a soul upward, there is an open window into eternity. Wherever the human spirit strives to push back the skirts of darkness and to widen the area of light, wherever men sacrifice their immediate interests of the one for the diviner aims of the life of the many together, there God is present in that search for the better and more inclusive world that is to be. The kingdoms we build for love's sake, our dedications to the good of the whole, our passions and agonizing struggles for light and truth and life are ways of touching the hem of the garment of God.

Measurements and descriptions, however true and accurate they may be, and however significant they may be as pointers, are bound to be accounts made from the outside. It is as though a spectator were trying to hint to our thought what is going on in the mind of a man by measuring the velocities and plotting the curves and spirals of molecular vibrations in the cortex of his brain. The diagram of movements may be perfect, and the cyclonic storm of neuron-waves may be minutely described. But no diagrammatic account tells the true story of what is actually in the mind of the man. The gateway into his secret is not through his neurons, but through an inner contact with his mind. If we are to find God it will not be with telescopes that search the stars and nebulae, nor with microscopes that reveal the infinitely small, nor with scalpels that dissect nerves and brain tissue. The gateway will be through love and truth and beauty and the will to make the good prevail; for these precious things can exist only through the mediation of another kind of world than that of masses of matter. And in the direct processes of the deeper life of the spirit we find ourselves in mutual and reciprocal correspondence with that Other Spirit who is God.

CHAPTER VIII

OPEN RELIGION AND SOME OF ITS PROBLEMS

HAS revelation ceased, or does God still speak to those who listen? Are the returns all in, or is revelation of spiritual truth continuous? Throughout the entire history of Christianity there have been two views of this matter, and consequently there have been claimants for two diverse types of authority. The authority of a divinely established, spiritually endowed, infallible Church has steadily held the dominant place, but on the other hand there has always been a claim for the authority of individual experience felt to be under the guidance of the Holy Spirit. They seem like two incompatible strains of inheritance. One seems bound to cancel out the other. How can the authoritative bishop or ordained priest keep house comfortably with the inspired "prophet" who speaks by sudden inspiration?

How can the authority of infallible Scripture leave scope and sphere for new illumination and guidance, for fresh light to break forth, as John Robinson of Leyden believed it would do? How can the authority of the Church be maintained and still at the same time leave the individual soul its free access to God through the ever-present Spirit? Can the Church preserve the authority of corporate organization, and at the same time leave freedom for the exercise of spiritual gifts, conferred upon individual members? These questions of Authority are as old as the Christian Church itself. In fact, they are even much older. They are as old as religion is. They were, however, raised to new life and power when the Christian Church came to birth. Already in the second century an old Christian man said to Justin Martyr, "Pray above all things that the Gates of Light may be opened to you." And such questions have been living issues at every epoch since in the life of the Church.

These two strains of spiritual stock through the centuries have been ineradicable. I am not at present concerned with the first type of authority, the authority of infallible systems. It has its own interpreters and its own defenders aplenty. It may, however, be said in passing that *traditional* foundations of every kind have seriously crumbled and have become weak and tottering. This first type of authority, therefore, if it is to be enduring, must be based on something essential and intrinsic, not upon a kind of "magic spell," or upon the glorification of the phrase, "it has always been so." Infinite "regressions" into the past prove to be weak supports for truth.

The second type of authority, the authority of individual inspiration or of guidance, is always in need of interpretation and of defense. It never has too many understanding friends or too great a retinue of intelligent supporters. The dangers involved in it, and the capricious features of it, are obvious to every one who is not himself swept along by the exuberance of prophetic "enthusiasm." If immediate guidance, direct inspiration, is to be one of the permanent strains in the constructive spiritual life of the world, it must pass through tests and sifting processes, and it must be able to verify its claims. In any case it is one of the most ancient manifestations of human experience, and it has its "spell of antiquity" quite parallel to that of the other type of authority.

Henri Bergson in his last book, *Les Sources de la Morale et de la Religion,* now translated with the title, *Morality and Religion,* which is a fitting crown of his life work of genius, holds that there are two types of ethics and two types of religion. There is, first, closed morality which is morality based on instincts and habits, customs and conventions. It hems life in with rules and regulations and makes it "safe" and calculable. It consists of rights and duties. It is conservative and static. Then, on the higher level there is "open morality," which is born through fresh insights and openings that come to transcendent persons. It is intuitive, creative, progressive and revolutionary. It is the result of fresh bursts of life breaking in from beyond the old levels.

It is initiated by persons who feel the surge of a tide of life—an *élan vital*—from above and beyond themselves. One is motived by fear, the other by love.

There is, again, he holds, a similar situation with religion. There are religions of the primitive and naturalistic type, fashioned out of fears and frustrations. Religions of this sort are characterized by rites and performances which gave, and perhaps still give, a sense of safety and security to the frightened child of humanity. Then there is an "open" or dynamic type of religion which is born from direct contact with the creative stream of divine Life. It brings a palpitating sense that the human and the divine have come together in a vital way. There is an intuition of depth which takes us to the very roots of our being and thus to the very basis of Life itself. The window of divine surprise is open. With this intuition of depth come complete spiritual health, abounding joy and enthusiasm for life. Humanity, half-crushed by the weight of its own progress and its mechanisms of civilization, can be saved only by thus entering the central Life-stream where it can refresh and restore itself. The line, I am sure, cannot be as sharply drawn as this account would seem to imply between the two types of morality and the two types of religion, but the difference between the lowest level of the one and the highest level of the other is like the difference in distance from here to the nearest street lamp and that from here to Orion.

I am concerned here only with Bergson's second type of religion, "open religion." By "open religion," as we have seen, he means religion which has direct contact with the creative stream of divine Life, the refreshment and restoration of the soul by an infusion of the Life of God. Consciousness of invasion, of rapture, of enthusiasm, of mystic opening, of oracular communication, is older than human records. It has always had its peculiar fascination for the recipient of such experiences, and it has apparently given its possessors a certain quality of personal influence over others. The feeling of contact with a superior power at once heightens the dynamic quality of a person's life, and naturally produces a quickened response of faith in those who have intimate dealings with such vitalized lives. Tennyson in *The Holy Grail* has beautifully described the way in which the holy maid who had *seen and felt* produced a spell on Sir Galahad:

> *As she spake*
> *She sent the deathless passion in her eyes*
> *Through him, and made him hers, and laid her mind*
> *On him, and* he believed in her belief.

In the simpler stage of human society, when tests were few and inexact, there were powerful temptations to assume such gifts when they did not actually exist, or to trade upon them when they did exist, and such enthusiasts often became a nuisance, if not a social menace. It soon became evident that they had to be controlled by another and more effective type of corporate authority. Slowly the scribe and the ordained official crowded the prophet into the background. The collision of these two types of authority has produced some of the major tragedies of history.

The Greek mystery cults gave large opportunity for mystical ecstasy and enthusiasm. It was their central doctrine that man's soul is of divine origin and is akin to the upper heavenly world. That belief naturally heightened the expectation of incursions from beyond the world of time and space, and encouraged the hope for divine guidance and spiritual direction from above. The impact of the mystery religions on the western world is, as everybody now knows, a significant story. Their influence on Socrates and Plato, and on the entire Platonic stream, is unmistakable. And there can be as little question that, not only in terminology but in deeper aspects as well, they left their mark upon the long line of Christian mysticism.

Another important strand of influence came through the Old Testament. There were many stages of "prophecy" among the Hebrew people. The earliest forms of it were marked by trance or ecstasy of the type described in the *Book of Numbers* in the Balaam narrative, "seeing the vision, falling down and having his eyes open" (Num. 24:4). Only gradually the great type of Hebrew prophecy emerged. It was the highest peak of the Hebrew genius. Prophecy in its noblest range did not dispense with the intellect or with the personality of the prophet. The inspiration which came upon the greatest of the prophets from the eighth to the sixth centuries B.C. elevated, sublimated and consecrated all the mental and spiritual powers of personality of these great prophets, who put all their personal gifts at the service of the will of God. This highest type of prophecy was, too, marked throughout its history by immense social passion.

Philo of Alexandria in the first century of our era, one of the most famous Jews in the history of that race, returned to the more primitive conception of inspiration. He thought of it as an ecstatic event, by which a divine "possession" replaced the original personality. "The mind in us," he says, "is removed from its place at the arrival of the divine," and the individual person becomes a passive instrument of the invading divine power. This position of Philo's glorifies the doctrine of the "broken and empty vessel," and it assumes that all that is human must withdraw before the divine Spirit can enter or can work effectively.

The experience of "gifts" in the early Church, as described especially in Acts and in First Corinthians, appears to have been of this ecstatic type. "Tongue-speaking," interpretation of tongues, messages given by "prophets," seem to have been "invasions" rather than the heightened normal expressions of spiritual life through enriched personality. Charismata, i.e., "gifts," as St. Paul uses the word, implies a superadded grace or power, bestowed upon the individual by special divine favor. It is the coming of something superadded from above; not the raising to higher quality of a capacity already possessed by the individual. St. Paul and St. John on the other hand for the most part are themselves extraordinary illustrations of the supremely great prophet who is raised by inspiration, not "out of himself," but rather to a unique level of life and power, so that the kindled personality becomes a living organ of the Spirit.

In the outbreak of Montanism which occurred in the second and third centuries, and which claimed to be the beginning of the new and final dispensation, the dispensation of the Holy Spirit, the "new prophecy" was, once more, definitely ecstatic, and the ideal state to be attained was one in which the "prophet" was "like a lyre" and the Holy Spirit was "like the plectrum which strikes the strings of the lyre." Whatever "revelation" came from God on this theory was believed to have come through the completely self-emptied and passive instrument of the person. The transmitter was like a hollow tube. That situation, once more, was true of the type of prophecy which was "revived" in the twelfth century by Joachim of Fiori, and by his followers, the "spiritual" Franciscan apostles of "the eternal Gospel."

The Christian mystics, who form an almost unbroken line from the writers of the New Testament to the present day, show both tendencies, the ecstatic type and also what I have been calling "the heightened normal type of revelation through enriched personality." Frequently, as we should expect, both of these types appear alternately in the same person, that is, in a given mystic. It should be said, however, that the greatest of the mystics, Eckhart, Ruysbroeck, Tauler, and St. Teresa, discounted the value of what we now call "psychic phenomena," or seemingly miraculous signs and occurrences. They put their main emphasis on moral and spiritual transformation of life and character. "God can no more do without us," Eckhart says, "than we can do without Him." And again, "The intellect never rests until it is filled full to its capacity." St. Teresa in her *Autobiography* says that her mystical experiences brought her "a harvest of ineffable spiritual riches and an admirable renewal of bodily strength." "All those who knew me," she says, "saw that I was changed. This improvement, palpable in all respects, far from being hidden, was brilliantly evident to all men." Ruysbroeck, the great Flemish mystic, maintained that the discovery of God brings "fecundity of life." And he declared that "every virtuous act presupposes a meeting with God." There is a fine saying in his *Ladder of Love* which emphasizes the way the values of life are heightened; "Love the Love that loves you everlastingly, for the more you love, the more you desire to love. When we hold fast by love, God by His Spirit remakes us and then His joy is ours."

Nevertheless, all these mystics had moments when they insisted that God cannot come in unless man "goes out"; and that "where the creature stops God begins." There is always a sense in which this self-negation is true. The narrow egoism of instinctive desires must be "killed." The conceit of superiority must be annihilated. There is no great spiritual life possible until we make the discovery that not what we "want," but what "God wills" is the way of life. Christ discovered in Gethsemane that what he wanted most—to "have the cup pass"—was not going to happen. The course of the world, the eternal laws of the kingdom of love, were not to be changed to meet his wishes, but his own *will* was to be changed to fit God's mind. That is the secret of the agony in the garden, and the secret of all our spiritual crucifixions. When we pray for "the Kindly Light to lead us we are not to expect it to lead us only the way we *want* to go. We need not be surprised to find Eckhart saying that no one can attain to the school of the Holy Spirit, "so long as he retains of nether things as much as a needle-point can carry." And we may find genuine wisdom in the insistence of the greatest mystics that there is a "dark night" to be passed through. In his noble drama, *Murder in the Cathedral,* T. S. Eliot has Archbishop Thomas à Becket, the martyr, say: "A martyrdom is never the design of man; for the true martyr is he who has become the instrument of God, who has lost his will in the will of God, not lost it but found it, for he has found freedom in submission to God. The martyr no longer desires anything for himself, not even the glory of martyrdom."

In the Reformation period a group of men who united the mystical strain with the intellectual impulse which came from Erasmus endeavored to effect a spiritual reformation of Christianity. The prevailing tendency of this little group of "spiritual reformers" in the sixteenth and seventeenth centuries was to build an invisible Church rather than a visible one. The inward word and light of God in man's soul was the ground of their faith and they aimed to spiritualize the normal, everyday life. Their favorite text was the saying in the Book of Proverbs: "The spirit of man is a candle of the Lord" (Prov. 20:27). This was taken by the spiritual reformers to mean that man's spirit can be lighted by God's Spirit and can become a revealing place for His light and life and love. These men inclined to the view that God through His Spirit inspires and heightens the capacities of a human soul and uses the person thus transformed as His organ of revelation and service.

Jacob Boehme (1575–1624), who is by far the most important person in this long line of humanistic-mystical interpreters of life, put this position of the human person as an organ of revelation as clearly as it can be stated. He said: "I must die with my outward man, (my self-centered will) in Christ's death and arise and live anew in Him. Therefore, I live now by the will of faith in the spirit of Christ and receive Christ with His humanity into my will. He makes through me a manifestation of the spiritual world and *introduces the true Love-sound into the harp-strings of my life.* He became that which I am and now He has made me that which He is!" (*Signatura rerum* XII. 10–13). Boehme, like most of the major mystics, had ecstatic experiences and felt himself to be carried beyond himself, but it is the main current of his testimony that man can be spiritualized, *enchristed,* and formed into a transmitting centre of the life and love of God here in the world.

This view of human life as a revealing organ of God was taken up and interpreted with great beauty and power in England by the Cambridge Platonists in the seventeenth century. Benjamin Whichcote is the father of the group. "Religion," this noble spiritual inter- preter says, "is not a system of doctrine, an observance of Modes or a Form of Words; *it is a frame and temper of mind;* it shows itself in a Life and Action comform- able to the Divine Will." For him true religion is a "nativity from above," the formation of a frame and temper of mind which governs all actions of life and conversation. "We naturalize ourselves," according to his great phrase, "We naturalize ourselves to the employment of eternity." "Heaven is a temper of spirit before it is a place."

John Smith, Whichcote's saintly disciple, "was lent by God," as his friends put it, "to the world for about five and thirty years." No one has better expressed than he the fact that the truest type of revelation is the life itself. This is his testimony: "Should a man hear a Voice from Heaven or see a Vision from the Almighty to testifie unto him the Love of God towards him; yet methinks it were more desirable to find a Revelation of all *from within,* arising up from the Bottome and Centre of a man's own soul, in the Reale and internal impressions of a Godlike nature upon his own spirit; and thus to find the Foundation and Beginning of Heaven and Happiness within himself; it were more desirable to see the crucifying of our own will, the mortifying of the meere Animal life, and to see a Divine Life rising up in the room of it, as a sure Pledge and inchoation of immortality and Happiness, the very Essence of which consists in a perfect conformity and cheerful compliance of all the Powers of our Souls with the Will of God." We do not roll out such sentences as that in our modern English style, nor do we often pack so much thought and wisdom into our words. Simon Patrick preached Smith's funeral sermon and in the course of it said: "God hath alwaies in the world men of greater height and stature than others, whom he sets up as torches on an hill to give light to all the regions round about." That word of Patrick's gives the essence of this humanistic-mystical principle that the best revelation in the world is the kindled and transformed life of a person.

The Quaker movement which burst like hot lava into activity when the Cambridge Platonists were quietly proclaiming their profound interpretations of life was both catastrophic and calm, both psychic and normal.[1] It gave evidence of both types of revelation—a direct opening from God as a "given" revelation, and the quiet testimony of a life made new by God's power and kindled into flame as a burning and a shining light. These two views alternate throughout the entire Quaker movement and have remained parallel rather than reconciled. It carried on many of the deep quiet mystical aspirations of the spiritual reformers to whom it owed its birth and it had in it just as certainly a startlingly "apocalyptic" tendency. Many of the early Quakers looked for divine "invasions." They looked for miracles of intervention. They expected supernatural "events" to burst into the time-order through them and to alter the course of history. They emphasized once more, as the Montanists had done in the second and third centuries, a type of ministry usually called "prophecy," which does not mean foretelling, but rather means speaking messages *given* ready-made to the speaker by "immediate inspiration."

[1] The dates of George Fox, its founder, were 1624–1691.

There was in the early Quaker gatherings a tremulous expectation on the part of the members that such messages would come, and that both the words and the substance of the message would be "given" to the speaker. Preparation for speaking was for this reason disapproved. The mind was to be quiescent and empty and the looked-for "message" was thought of in the nature of a "communication" to the speaker and through him to the people. The powerful influence of French Quietism on the Quakerism of the eighteenth century heightened still further this "empty vessel" conception of ministry. It came to be the prevailing view of ministry and prayer in Quaker circles, and all approved Quaker preaching took the form of "rapt" utterance, which was believed to be the transmission of communications "given" to the speaker for the occasion. The Inward Light was thus raised to a miraculous level and was thought of as a supernatural and infallible vehicle for the manifestation here on earth of truths and openings which could have originated only in a supernal world.

The other, and the saner, view of inspiration, however, was never lost in the stream of the Quaker movement. The early founders of the movement, especially Fox and Penn, had an exalted faith that there is "something of God in every man." They called this "something of God" by various names—"the immortal Seed," "the Light," "the Truth," "the Spirit," or "the Christ within." They meant that man is something more than his natural, temporal, finite self. They interpreted man as more than "mere man," as a being who could either live upward toward God or downward toward earth, a being essentially amphibious—made to live in either one of two worlds. Fox certainly in his early period when he was breaking his way with dynamic effect, was the bearer of this great faith that God and man in his inmost depth are unsundered. "I had come up," he said, "through the flaming sword into the paradise of God, to the state Adam was in before he fell." "Christ renews men," he says again, "into the image of God which men and women were in before they fell." In his greatest discovery he says: "I saw that there was an ocean of darkness and death; but I saw that there was an infinite ocean of light and love that flowed over the ocean of darkness." This is an optimism born of the faith and the experience that neither man as man, nor the universe itself, is insulated from God.

This glowing insight of Fox champions the faith that at our highest and best and truest attainment of life, we reveal the fact of something infinite and transcendent breaking through our finite lives. We discover the eternal in the midst of our temporal moments. We can live up toward the enveloping inclusive Life of the Spirit to which *we belong*. We can find the Ocean of light and love flowing over our scenes of darkness and death. We can become transmissive instruments of this More above us and in us, which we rightly call God, our Life and Light.

That serene and quiet view of the relation between God and man is the original Quaker strand which I wish had won the dominant place in the history of the movement. It holds that man and God belong together. It conceives of personality as both a divine and a human creation. Man's life can be purified and raised to an intimate correspondence with God and can become a radiant centre, a luminous point, through which God shows what human life really means. This view that God is both transcendent and immanent, is a vastly important truth. It means that while God is more than can ever be expressed in a world of space and time, He is nevertheless genuinely present here in our world as Spirit meeting with our spirits and transmuting our human lives into transmissive organs of His will and purpose. If the Quakers had consistently interpreted this position and had consistently illustrated it in their lives, as in fact they often did, they would have made a major contribution to the spiritual life of the modern world.

Their long-continued emphasis on a type of ministry which assumed that the mind must be empty and un-prepared and that the words must be divinely "given" without any human contribution in the process, resulted in a neglect of culture and a belittling of the personal coefficient, and in a ministry which easily thinned out and degenerated. It is quite obvious that when the conscious self is "suppressed" and the individual will is "annihilated" what really happens is that the subconscious or submerged life—the hinterland beyond the frontier—comes into operation and the "message" that is delivered bears the unmistakable marks of the unconscious processes below the threshold of the person who gives it. What surges up from the deep well of the subconscious life is often rich with a wealth of experience and in rare souls it comes spontaneously formed and harmonized with touches of beauty and power, as one sees in the work of great geniuses. But there is no evidence that it is more divine, more supernatural, or more infallible, than is what comes in intelligent ways from the *whole* person who in his unified life possesses his normal powers of mind and thought.

The most genuine form of inspiration, then, will be, not that type which discounts the value of personality and expects "invasions" and "communications" from the utterly beyond, but that type which brings the divine Spirit and the human self into the truest and closest correspondence and coöperation. Man does not "go out" in order to have God "come in." Rather he humbly presents all that he is, the best that life and experience have done for him, all that has rolled up and accumulated of spiritual gain through the years of joy and sorrow, and lets the light and love of God radiate and break through his whole being both in its conscious and its unconscious levels.

A prism suddenly reveals to us something in the nature of a beam of light which we should never have suspected to be there if we had only known light in its pure radiance. It is so, I believe, with the nature and character of God. We cannot be *perfect* transmitters of such infinitely transcendent reality as the nature of God. We are bound even when we are at our best to distort and color the divine radiance which breaks through us, as the prism does the beam of light, but something of God which the world would miss if we did not perform our mission as transmitters does come through. Our human love often seems imperfect and weak, but genuine human love bestowed in simple spontaneous ways for love's sake is a revelation of a love which has its true source only in God. It is so with truth and beauty and goodness. We can show these supreme realities of life only in human finite measures, but every time we succeed in transmitting any tiny facet of truth, any gleam of the beauty of life, any demonstration of triumphant good-will, something of God's eternal nature has been expressed in the world of time. The tiny branches of the great Vine have thus revealed the life and spirit which circulates in the eternal Vinestock itself. Evelyn Underhill in *The Golden Sequence* has given a beautiful illustration of this divine-human coöperation which I should like to quote:

"There is on the north porch of the Cathedral of
Chartres a wonderful sculpture of the creation of Adam.
There we see the embryonic human creature, weak,
vague, half-awakened, not quite formed, like clay on
which the artist is still working: and brooding over
him, with His hand on His creature's head, the strong
and tender figure of the Artist-Creator. Creative Love,
tranquil, cherishing, reverent of His material, in His
quiet and patient method: so much more than human,
yet meeting His half-made human creature on its own
ground, firmly and gradually moulding it to His unseen
pattern, endowing it with something of His own life.
It is a vision of the Old Testament seen in the trans-
figuring light of the New Testament. The *I will* of an
Absolute Power translated into the *I desire* of an Absolute Love; awful holiness reaching out to earthly weakness, and waking it to new possibilities. Now this situation is surely the situation of all living souls; and the
very essence of their spiritual life is or should be the
lifting up of the eyes of Adam, the not yet fully human
creature who is being made, in his weakness and hope,
to the holy creative love which never lets him go, and
in which his life is to find its meaning and goal."

This mystical relation between the soul of man and
the divine Spirit brings freshness and the power of personal conviction to the person who experiences it, but it
obviously does not make an individual an infallible
organ of revelation. The person is not turned into a

passive instrument of communication. He possesses his own peculiar traits of personal life. He has the marks of limitation which beset us all. He has his own specific mental outlook and his own psychological climate. He is bound to color with his own tinge the flow of truth and thought that comes through him.

> *Life like a dome of many colored glass*
> *Stains the white radiance of eternity.*

This is not a misfortune or a limitation to be fought against. It is an essential feature of life incident to personality. To become the ecstatic type of revealer one would be compelled to give up what is most precious to us and what must also be most precious to God; namely all that we mean by experience, all that we have gained by pain and love, all that goes to make us *us*. That would turn us into a non-personal and wholly mysterious instrument of transmission. Persons in all ages have strained after that condition and have yearned for miraculous communications. But the history of mysticism, and especially the history of the Quaker movement, indicates that the essential spiritual contributions have been those which have come through kindled and heightened personalities in their normal processes of life rather than those which came in the form of mysterious communications when the individual's mind was "absent."

I have been severely disillusioned by the automatic

writing and automatic speaking which have frequently come under my notice. Many authors have sent me manuscripts which have been automatically "given" to them, but they possess very slight value for the human race and clearly indicate that when the intelligent and conscious life of the person is suppressed there is a distinct drop in the worth of the communication which results, not a rise to a unique or infallible level. It lacks the mature wisdom, the selective insight and the balance of judgment of the integrated and unified self.

Karl Barth, disillusioned by the vagaries of psychology and shaken awake by the pantheistic interpretations of divine immanence, with its cosmic urges, its *libidos* and its *élans vitals,* has formulated a crisis-theology of retreat and gone back to an excessive doctrine of transcendence which makes God's nature and character forever unrevealable in terms of human life or thought or historical movements. God for him is so completely and absolutely other, *Ganz Anders,* that He is beyond all that our minds can think or our agonizing hearts can feel.

> *Whatever your mind comes at*
> *I tell you flat*
> *God is not that.*

This position surrenders the faith that we are fellow-laborers with God and that there is a victory which overcomes the old world and rebuilds the new one ac-

cording to the divine pattern. It chills forever the hope
that "Spirit with spirit may meet." It leaves us in an
undivine world and with no east windows opening to
the Light.

On the other hand it will not do to assume that God
has special favorites whom he relieves from the labor
of thinking and whom He supplies with comfortable
directions denied to other mortals, or that any idea
which happens to come suddenly and mysteriously into
the mind is *ipso facto* divinely given. The suddenness
of their coming and the urgency of their presence have
always given a peculiar importance to ideas and insights which *burst* upon the mind, but neither suddenness nor urgency is an adequate test. We know too
much now about the way the submerged deeps within
us operate to allow us to call everything which shoots
across the margins of consciousness a heavenly revelation. There must be some adequate principle of selection, some clear mark of distinction if we are to submit
our lives to private intimations of "guidance," and if
we are to grant an august authority to our "divine lead-
ings," either for speech or for action. Ready-made,
specific "communications," automatically presented to
the mind, almost invariably reveal the formative operation of a person's subconscious life. There may be
something more in them than has originated in the
private life of the individual, but they must not be
forthwith accepted as "communications" solely on the

ground that the mind has not produced them by conscious effort.

It seems in every way probable that the interior life of the individual is in immediate contact with environing Spirit and may draw upon the spiritual energies within its reach for inspiration and fortification, for heightening the quality of its life and for widening its scope and range, but it looks as though there were always a human factor present as soon as specific interpretation occurs, or as soon as definite formulation begins. In other words, I incline to the view that what comes from beyond us is in the nature of contact, sense of presence, inflooding of energy, heightening of the quality of life, increase of dynamic, rather than ready-made "communications." And I further believe that the effect is richer when the whole self is unified, with all the powers of the mind coöperatively working with the subconscious life, than when the subconscious life automatically presents its product ready-made to the passive mind.

We may turn finally to consider how such high-tide experiences of the soul are to be tested. There are no exact mathematical tests, there is no "spiritometer," by which incoming energies of the Spirit can be measured. There is, however, an inward witness by which all that is divinest in us recognizes the divine guest and answers back with the joyous cry of *Abba*—deep calling unto deep. It is the burning of the heart in a communion that is too inward to be translated into outward proof. For one who has the experience it has the same evidence that love ever has—the evidence of recognition and response. This inward witness, however, if it is to be recognized as a divine gift, must forthwith reveal its truth in the spiritual transformation which it effects in the individual's life. The highest traits of character we know in God are love, gentleness, tenderness and self-giving grace. Where the meeting of the soul with God brings forth such fruits in the life of a person as those, we may well believe the evidence. Where love is, God is. He that dwelleth in love dwelleth in God. Transmutation of the inward spirit of a person is one form of demonstration. It is the pure in heart that see God and purity of heart means gentleness, kindliness, tenderness, sympathetic understanding as well as freedom from those impurities which blur the soul's vision.

But the inward spirit must also produce outward effects. When there is a genuine inward "witness" that the guest has come in, the transmutation of spirit must go forth into newness of life-relationships. There must be a transfusion of the spirit into the field of action. As the quality of faith rises the whole life becomes enriched and deepened by it and a corresponding ethical quality blossoms forth into flower and fruit. One cannot be sure that the tides of the mystic Ocean have surged into his inmost life until he finds himself possessed with a new and deeper passion to have his life turned into a living radiation-centre of the Kingdom of God which is forever being built where Christ is present. The seal of the authority which divine inspiration gives is measured by the quality of demonstration and power revealed thereby in the life of the individual. It is a severe test, but it is the only certain one.

It is no accident that the two most powerful trends of present-day Christianity are a fresh revival of mystical religion and an awakened passion to carry Christianity into the fabric and tissue of the social life of humanity. We shall never again be satisfied with a salvation which promises peace and comfort only after death. We want a gospel which makes here and now a world where love and peace await a new-born child. "We must turn all we possess into the channel of universal love."

St. Augustine wrote his *civitas dei* while the greatest empire the world has ever seen was crashing down around him. More truly than any other man he produced the basic plan on which the world that emerged out of the ruin was built. Once more we find ourselves forced, whether we like the task or not, to be rebuilders of a world that has fallen to pieces around us. The task seems to many persons to be primarily that of discovering the right social and economic order. And that quite obviously must be the task in the foreground, but we shall find, as St. Augustine found, that whatever may be the social structure in which men are to live, the deepest question, the ultimate question, will still be, what is it that makes a life intrinsically good and eternally worth while as a spiritual unit in the social order that is to be built?

Chapter IX

SOUL–FORCE

MAHATMA GANDHI has made our generation very familiar with the phrase *soul-force.* His native word for it is *Satyagraha,* which is often loosely translated "non-violence." That negative phrase, however, only feebly expresses the positive significance of the original Indian word. Gandhi has steadily maintained that *truth* and *love,* exhibited undeviatingly in a life purified from fear, hate, injustice, and bitterness, are invincible forces of the soul, and that is essentially what he means by "soul-force." He said to me in 1926: "Faith in the conquering power of love and truth has gone all the way through my inmost being and nothing in the universe can ever take it from me."

St. Francis of Assisi concentrated all the energies of his life on the interpretation of love in action. He said less than Gandhi has said of the significance of *truth.* But love for Francis always involved consistency, sincerity, and loyalty to the highest which his soul apprehended. Although he did not talk so much of *truth* as Gandhi has done, his life rang true and his supreme soul-force—*love*—included the quality of truth. It would not be easy to find a more sublime scene than that of this thin emaciated *poverello* standing in chains before the Soldan of the Moslem world and telling him, what all the armies of the Crusaders could never have made him believe, that Christ came to reveal love and light, and had sent him, alone and unafraid, to be the messenger of love, the bearer of the way of peace.

Chesterton, with his usual happy way of flashing out an unforgettable phrase, says that "Francis ran away to God, as other boys run away to sea." And that discovery of God as love which Francis made, or rather the rediscovery of it as a vital reality to live by, is what made St. Francis such a centre of spiritual energy in the thirteenth century. *The Little Flowers* tells how he got out of bed one night and "with exceeding great fervour" said: " 'My God, my God,' and naught beside!" until morning, feeling himself drawn into a living communion with the Source of Love. At Alverna he prayed: "O Lord, my Saviour, I ask two favors before I die. Let me feel in my soul, in my body even, all the bitter pains which Thou hast felt. And in my heart let me feel that immeasurable love which made Thee, Son of God, endure such sufferings for us, poor sinners."

The secret of his soul-force was this union of child with Father and the birth in him of "immeasurable love." Gandhi, in a different way, by the path of Indian mysticism, bases his doctrine of soul-force upon the power of the human soul to be an organ of that one Reality behind all life. Mysticism is always bold, but Indian mysticism is peculiarly daring. It has held for more than two thousand years, through its greatest exponents that there is an interior depth to the human soul which is in its essence uncreated and deathless. It is beyond the changes of "is and was and will be." It is absolutely real and inseparable from that eternal Reality that is the Root and Basis of all that is. After exhausting every method of expression and every ingenuity of thought to hint to human ears the nature of this deepest reality behind the temporal and fleeting things of the world, the Indian mystic is accustomed to end his account of the unutterable with the words, "*That* art thou." He identifies, in other words, the inmost being of his own self with the inmost Reality in the universe. At one point within what he calls himself, he believes that he enters, through a mysterious gateway, the realm of all that is Real, and he dares to say, "That am I." "That art thou."

His approach to reality is thus not through rocks and hills and skies, not through molecular forces and the energies of suns, not even through the sacred Himalayas, but through the reality which reaches the highest degree of certainty to him, the reality of his own mind. He begins, thus, not with books and documents, not with traditions and external authorities, but with the verity of conscious self-existence. The surest evidence that the universe culminates in a type of reality which can be called "spiritual" is to be found in the fact that when we penetrate "the labyrinthine ways of our own mind" we are already in the realm of the spirit.

We need a new "Depth Psychology" of quite a different order from that which the experts in abnormality and in sex perversions have been giving us. There is a large amount of reliable testimony, coming to us from all peoples that have a literature, that persons, often of unusual sanity and wisdom, have had invading contact in the depth of their souls with the central creative Stream of Life, and have thereby transcended the limitations of their species and have become dynamic centres of spiritual energy. There is no more reason for doubting the fact of such transformation than there is for doubting that iron plunged into the fire becomes itself transformed and penetrated with the fire, or that a needle of tempered steel may be magnetized until it becomes sensitive to the invisible magnetic currents which stream around it and can put itself into parallelism to them.

It seems only too obvious that the world which we see and touch is not an independent and self-sufficing substance. It carries in itself no explanation of itself. It is not *Maya*, an illusion or a shadow. It possesses some kind of reality. But there must be something more real and more truly self-explanatory beyond it, or in behind it, or interpenetrating it, if we could only get

in to find it. But always that inferred Reality "in behind," remains "in behind," and eludes us as the other
side of the moon does, the side which no one on earth
has ever seen. We are forced by the usual way of
approach to go from outside in and to *infer* the true
nature of the inmost Real from our observation of outside reality, which is always typically material stuff. It
is impossible to identify the most refined outward things
with what is "in behind," since the one is obviously
"material" and the other is assumed to be "spiritual,"
and we are always in danger of ending with the material, with which we began. We may perhaps find
that we can succeed better in our pursuit of the spiritually real if we begin with what is indubitably
spiritual to start with, the consciousness of our own
self-existence and proceed from what we ourselves are.

The mystical doctrine of the union of the soul at its
deepest centre with the Soul of the universe is perhaps
not explicitly present in Gandhi's idea of "soul-force,"
but he always implies that something vastly greater
than man's will or thought or scheme or plan flows
through the sincere and dedicated soul. The soul in its
depth has the moral and spiritual universe behind it.
The soul-centre of a pure, sincere person becomes, in
Gandhi's view of life, a fountain of love and truth and
wisdom, and when it keeps its selfish desires and its
individual aims in complete abeyance so that the stream
of life is pure, all the strength and love and truth of

God flow through the soul of the person of that type. The soul becomes, in fact, a channel of the infinite Reality and an extraordinary centre of energy. Emerson, as everybody knows, preached this doctrine of the soul as an organ of the Over-soul with serene eloquence, and was throughout his life, in the atmosphere of American practical realism, an untiring exponent of the exhaustless energy of man's soul in contact with the Over-soul.

This depth-view of the soul lies at the very heart of Johannine Christianity, though it is thought of there as an imparted gift of grace rather than as a native capacity: "He that shall drink of the water that I shall give him, it shall become in him a fountain of water springing up unto life eternal" (John IV, 14). Here the eternal source of the Life as Spirit floods into the human spirit and flows out through the human channel. The parable of the Vine and its branches illustrates vividly in a familiar figure a vital union of the individual person at his interior depth with the Eternal Vine-stock, in which, as a mighty Igdrasil Tree, the life-sap of the world has its home. And, once more, in exalted words we are told that when the Spirit of Truth comes into operation in the lives of men He will lead men into all the Truth" (John XVI, 13).

This doctrine of soul-force to which some of the noblest of our race have borne witness, however, flies pretty straight in the face of present-day psychological

theories of the soul. The "soul" has been passing
through a time of "depression" and seems to many persons "down and out." It takes courage even to be on
friendly terms with this poor outcast. Most writers
have stopped speaking of the soul, and some timid
preachers pause in their sermons to apologize for still
using "the bedraggled word."

But we need not be too much overawed in what concerns the deepest issues of life, by the conclusions of
modern psychology. Psychology is not yet at a stage
in its development when it can speak with authority or
lay down infallible laws for the control of our spirits.
It is bound to miss, as all scientific approaches do miss,
the inmost reality of things. The psychological approach to the problem of the soul and to all other
problems of life is in terms of description, and it still
remains on the outside. It treats the mind as a series
of events. Its basis of operation is that of an outside
spectator. Its method is observation. It accumulates and
interprets facts and processes of experience, not experience as it is felt. Genuine psychology, after the manner
of science in general, is modest in its claims and pre-
suppositions. It prescribes restraint. It endeavors to
keep within its limited field of description and observation of observed facts.

As soon as psychology goes beyond the sphere of
description of mental phenomena and enters upon that
of explanation, it usually inclines to a theory of brain

causation to account for mental facts. It also adopts the view that sensations are due to the impact of the external world upon the receptive organs of sense. Both of these theories obviously transcend observation. They both pass from actual experience to a metaphysical interpretation of it. It is no doubt the most obvious and natural form of explanation, but it is none the less metaphysical interpretation, not observation. Psychologists have taken this direction because it seemed to them to be the simplest one to take and because it was thought to involve a *minimum* of metaphysical theory.

But whether this method of explanation involves a *minimum* of metaphysics or not, it does, nevertheless, rest in the last analysis on metaphysical interpretation, not on observation. It is interpretation, not direct empirical approach. It transcends experience and it introduces something that has not been *observed* and something which from the nature of the case never can be *observed*. Furthermore, it has the disadvantage of laboring to explain a spiritual fact, a state of consciousness, a directly felt experience, by something wholly unlike it. There is nowhere else in the universe a parallel to the chasm between *a fact of conscious experience in the mind* and *molecular currents in the physical substance of the brain* that are assumed to be the "cause" of the conscious experience. Nor is there any possible way in sight of explaining how "impacts" of physical things in an external world could possibly produce consciousness of objects or, for that matter, any kind of mental states in a realm which is not physical.

No bridge over either of these chasms is yet known to us. We cross both chasms by a leap, and we leave the method of the "leap" unexplored. We go on talking as though molecular currents "produced" thought and as though outside "impacts" *caused* mental states, although our ignorance here is as deep as night. Some day a new Copernicus in the field of psychology will clarify the issue, and he will almost certainly clarify it by discovering that what we have been calling "physical" or "material" or "molecular" is vastly more interpenetrated by "spirit" than we have usually supposed. There is undoubtedly a remarkable "fit" between the inward and the outward. It is like the fit of the glove to the hand or like the two blades to a pair of scissors. The outward and the inward are certainly not divided by an absolute chasm. The object of our knowledge is not "an absolute other" to the mind that experiences it. They belong together as truly as do the convex and concave sides of a curve, and no man can "put them asunder." If we begin with a spiritual centre at the heart of our process of knowledge, we must be ready to go on and admit that there is a correspondent spiritual core within the universe itself.

But if we are to continue to use the word "soul," the word must be vitally re-interpreted, and it must be brought over into the language of current human speech. We cannot successfully revive the doctrine of the soul as a "spiritual substance," existing in solitary splendor, an entity of an order entirely unrelated to that of "extended substance." That doctrine leaves the soul in a realm of complete mystery. It becomes an "abstract" reality. We have no concrete data about it. We can never talk about it in any known terms, for all our words are "infected" with a pale cast of the world which we *experience*. The moment a reality is introduced into our conversation, which has no relation to experience, we are dumb in reference to it. The school man might debate how many angels could stand on the point of a needle, and Descartes might declare that the soul rested on the mathematical point at the tip of the pineal gland, but in both cases a definite *relation,* however refined and infinitesimal, was assumed to exist. As soon as all relation between the two realms is denied we must stop talking of one of them in terms of the other, for we find ourselves talking about something utterly outside and beyond the purview of thought or words. It is like the lost end of the Irishman's rope which somebody had "cut off."

If the soul is to be considered as a centre of spiritual energy, we must cease to think of it as an abstract entity unrelated to and "wholly other" than the world which we experience and know. It must be something capable of process, of growth and development. It must accumulate the gains of experience. It must be enriched by the disciplines of life. Otherwise it is and it remains a static entity, spinning functionlessly in a vacuum, no more fruitful at the end of a millennium than at the beginning of it. If one succeeded in getting such a soul as that "saved" it would hardly be worth saving, since it would be exactly what it was before it was "saved"!

Let us stop, then, trying to glorify the soul by making it an abstract entity, a "dark night in which all cows are black." The real soul which concerns a serious man, for which he would barter everything else and would fight the good fight and endure the perils to the uttermost, is his central self. Whatever more it may be, it is at least what it reveals itself to be. It is a centre of the consciousness of objects and at the same time of the consciousness of itself as knowing them. Every living pulse of our inner life reveals a knower and a something known in indivisible unity. At a later stage of experience, in retrospect, we may try to "explain" the known thing as though it were given to us from the outside, and we may talk of the knower as though it were an inside subject apart by itself. But in actual fact the knower and the known cannot be cut apart and be discovered in separation. Subject and object are always known together, like Shakespeare's lovers—"two distincts, division none." The soul as central self is an active organ of consciousness and also an organ of that

higher kind of consciousness which we call self-consciousness, that is to say, we can make the self an object
of thought and it can know itself as knowing.

It is not only active; it is creative as well. Every experience of so-called "given facts" is far more than
a *receptive* affair, as though the facts were "impressed,"
or "reported," or "stamped in," like stock prices on the
ticker tape. There are no "facts" that are facts for us
until we have *interpreted* what we are pleased to call
the *data* of our senses. A "pure sensation," that is a
sense experience uninfluenced by memory or association,
and uncolored by the mind's interpretation of what it
has received, is, as William James once put it, "as
mythological as the Jack of Spades." The moment life
reaches the stage of conscious experience it is forthwith *interpreted experience,* and our central self is, in
the process of interpretation, both active and creative.
The creative function of the mind in perception is a
process of bringing together the "reports" from the different senses—sight, hearing, touch, for instance—
fusing them with aspects supplied from memory, unifying all the details into one indivisible object and
interpreting it in terms of the universal class to which
it belongs. Our well-known tendency to *act* in reference to the situation is, too, an important, though
usually unrecognized, feature of the process by
which we discover and interpret the object in front
of us.

We set it, too, in a framework of space and time, and by processes too subtle for analysis, we put it in a definite class. We deal with it under a concept. Not to classify an object, for beings like us, is not to know it. Perception and conception are thus not two separable stages of the process of knowledge; they are one and indivisible, they go on together. All "particular" things which we perceive are what they are for us, because we recognize them as belonging to a universal class. They become *known* because they become *conceptualized*. If we lost our universal labels for the things we see or touch, we should lose the meaning of the particular objects themselves. So ingrained is this universalizing process that Plato has seemed to many of his readers to hold that we bring our universal ideas with us from the world in which we lived before birth, and here in this world we are reminded of them, or we "recollect" them, when we see objects of sense. The more modern way of putting this position of Plato's would be, that there is an inherent capacity of the mind by which we think the universal in the presence of the particular object, or that "particular" and "universal" are two aspects of one unanalyzable process of the mind when it is dealing with the reports of the senses —the "impacts" of the world.

In any case, however we phrase the process of knowledge, it is as truly an active and creative operation of mind as painting the Sistine Madonna was. Obliterate the centre of creative energy and you obliterate at the same time the possibility of knowing anything. Nearly everybody forgets or overlooks the marvelously complex *operation of the mind* in the process of knowing an object out there in the world. The object seems to be catapulted into the passive mind, or "impressed" upon it like a seal on wax. But that easy solution of the problem, in spite of the fact that John Locke fell for it, misses the actual facts of the case as surely and as widely as a blind man misses the fine points of a football game.

The creative work of the imaginative artist seems on the face of it more obviously to involve a centre of creative energy than the process of knowledge does. We are apt to think of actual truth as a correspondence with a reality that is there all the time, confronting us, and it seems easy to assume that the mind has passively received it as a "presentation," without doing anything itself. But it takes very little critical survey of the processes of the mind to settle the point that the organizing and unifying of experience from within, and its interpretation in terms of *meaning,* is a mental contribution of tremendous significance.

When we pass from the common experience of recognizing facts which are before us and of discovering their meaning, and pass on to consider what is involved in the knowledge of *truth,* we are at once carried to deeper levels of the creative energy of the soul, or mind, if one prefers the more modern word. There is no ticker-tape mechanism by which what we mean by *truth* could be stamped in from the outside. It is not a thing of the sense-order, furnished ready-made by the outside world. *Truth* has universal and absolute reference. If it is seen at all, it is seen to be *inevitably* so. It resists all attempts to think the opposite of it. It has been humorously said that the modern doctrine of relativity means that "there is no hitching post in the universe." But it is impossible to obliterate from the universe this one particular "hitching post"—the stability of *truth*. The theory of "relativity" itself involves precisely that kind of stability. That theory is either true or it is not true. If it is true, then it possesses an absolute stability—a stability which will abide until new facts compel a reformation of the theory to conform with *truth*. The "hitching post" is still there. If the theory itself is not true, then the argument from relativity vanishes, and the truth abides as of old. There is something in the nature of *truth* which is determined not by the coming and going of facts, or by the relativity of things in space and time, but by the *nature of the mind that does the knowing*. The "hitching post" is not somewhere outside, so that it may eventually be passed by and left behind in "the process of the suns"; it is in the soul of man and will abide as long as the reality of knowledge abides. So long as any person is left in the world who can stand up and say, *I know,* there will be indisputable evidence of a central self, which is what a modern man means by the "soul."

But the mind has another approach to reality which reveals the interior depth of the soul and its unique creative activity in an even more impressive way. There are rare persons of the genius type who *see with their minds* some larger truth which must be real in order to complete what is already known to be true, though they have before them at the moment no observable sense facts which are adequate to prove or verify it. They anticipate this larger truth the way a mathematician sees the whole curve needed to complete a tiny arc, or the way a zoölogist sees in a single fossil bone what the nature of the extinct animal must have been and what kind of an environment was needed to support its life. Goethe saw how Strasbourg Cathedral would need to be finished if it were to be architecturally consistent with what its architect, Erwin of Steinbach, built. The discoverer of Neptune saw with his mind the solar system could not be a consistent universe without another planet beyond the orbit of Uranus. There were, however, in these instances, no sense facts present at the time to confirm and verify what the mind anticipated. Such truths could be discovered only by a mind of sufficient range and depth to hold many facts together, to see their significance, and then to leap beyond them to possibilities of experience never yet presented to sense, to see them in imagination and then to prepare the way to demonstrate their reality.

In the case of the greatest souls there is a moral insight which is almost as unerring as is the insight by which the astronomer plots the path of a total solar eclipse months or years ahead of the event. For such persons the vision of the ideal of advance, at least so far as it concerns their own deeds is, or may become, the main driving force of their lives. They see so clearly what is needed to accomplish the next stage, that they build on ahead of all that has yet been done, and produce a new and unique achievement, which but for their vision would have been impossible. It has been well called "a conviction of things not seen."

But our real life as persons is always deeper than our consciousness ever reveals. The central stream of our being is too deep for any of our present sounding lines to fathom it.

Beneath the stream, shallow and light, of what we say
    we feel,
Beneath the stream, as light, of what we think we feel,
There flows with noiseless current, obscure and deep,
The central stream of what we are *indeed.*

William James gave this impressive account of this submerged life in his *Varieties of Religious Experience:* [1]

[1] William James: *Varieties of Religious Experience,* p. 483. By permission of Longmans, Green & Co.

"It is," he said, "an exhaustless fountain head, ever pouring out fresh conceptions as from some unseen laboratory; the abode of everything that is latent, the reservoir of everything that passes unrecorded and unobserved. It contains, for example, such things as our momentarily inactive memories, and it harbors the springs of all our obscurely motived passions, impulses, likes, dislikes and prejudices; our intentions, hypotheses, fancies, superstitions, persuasions, convictions and, in general, all our non-rational operations come from it. It is the source of our dreams and apparently they may return to it. In it arise whatever mystical experiences we may have, and our automatisms, sensory and motor; our life in hypnotic or hypnoid conditions; our delusions, fixed ideas and hysterical accidents, if we are hysterical subjects." That interesting inclusive summary which James has given by no means tells the whole story. All creative work which attains a high degree of perfection is gestated in the deeps of the subconscious. Professor Livingston Lowes in *The Road to Xanadu* has thrown a flood of light upon the way the two most metrically perfect poems of Coleridge, "Ancient Mariner" and "Kubla Khan," were silently formed in what he calls the "deep well of the poet's sub-conscious mind" out of the scraps, the detritus, deposited there from a long list of books of travel which the poet had recently read. They were fused and forged into perfect form by the kindling heat of the poet's imagination, and the poems seemed to surge up out of the deep-level wealth of his life. A. C. Bradley, in his *Oxford Lectures on Poetry,* has shown conclusively that Shakespeare's greatest dramatic passages came to birth in a similar fashion from the raw material which was latent in his mind, from previous reading. It all seemed to be done with the ease of an angel waving a wand. The greatest orators report that their supreme achievements seemed at the moment to be given to them by a power beyond themselves. Something "wells up" by an *élan mystique* and is "presented," perfectly formed for the purpose. This submerged life of ours must not be thought of merely as a deep sub-cellar from which hysterical phenomena emerge, and where the demons of complexes and fears dance their wild mazes. It is as well a realm of inspirations and the source of all our perfect performances.

The word, *Mneme,* has been coined to cover all "the deep well" gains of life which are stored up through the principle of conservation, by memory, by habit, by practice, and by adaptation. It is what we usually mean by "second nature" processes. All work done under the immediate direction of attention is slow, inaccurate and exhausting. Think, for example, intently of how to make your letters and at once your handwriting looks as it used to in your early copy-books. Turn the sentence over to your submerged life and away the hand goes in easy and graceful movements. As soon as you call upon the trained submerged powers you have the simple accuracy of instinct, and your performance becomes swift, sure and easy. One can always tell whether he is winning excellence by the ease with which he performs his tasks or his duties. The ease of excellence is, however, bought at a great price. It has cost labor and toil. It is the fruit of concentration and persistent effort. This is the way spirit conquers nature. "That is not first which is spiritual, but that which is natural, and afterward that which is spiritual." This all has significant bearing on the moral life of a man. Nobody is thoroughly good until he has formed his resolutions into habits and has carried his duties beyond the stage of effort—until he does what is right "without thinking." The Psalmist praises the man who has "truth in his inward parts." Aristotle selects as his best moral specimen the person who has attained "moral dexterity of will." Clement of Alexandria finds his highest type of life in "the harmonized man," who through action and the practice of insight has attained a rightly fashioned tendency to act, and who has moral poise and decision wrought into the inward structure of his life.

Beneath these inward deeps that are revealed in the processes of knowledge, in the discovery of truth, in the forereach of creative imagination, in the moral response to what ought to be and in "second nature" processes there is an uncreated root or ground, an in-

most centre of the soul, a centre of profound quiet out
of which is born a vital energizing of the whole being.
All of us who live richly have moments when we drop
below the thin surface of life and find the deeps of
repose, where what we do springs out of what we are.
The contemplative spirit of Mary and the activity of
Martha are here fused into a single unity. At the centre
of unmoved repose there is a union of quiet peace which
passes understanding with an amazing tension of concentrated energy. Eckhart in the fourteenth century
compared this central repose to the hinge of a door.
The door opens and shuts, is moved to and fro, but the
hinge itself all the time remains unmoved and un-
moving.

For the great mystics of all ages and of all faiths
the original core of man's being is this interior depth of
the soul—the *Ultima Thule* of the personal self, below
the level of conscious striving or the disturbing maladies
of the temporal life. The "mystical wonder," which is
as indescribable as the surge of feelings which flood the
beholder of the Grand Canyon, comes from the quiet
assurance that here in the centre of repose the finite
meets the infinite. There is a depth within where the
tiny part, often so sundered and ego-centred, touches
and is vitallized by the Life of the Whole. The roots
of our being become bathed with the currents of Life
from which we have sprung—"round our restlessness"
flows His rest.

The eye sinks inward, and the heart lies plain,
And what we mean, we say, and what we would, we know.

. . . . . .

And man becomes aware of his life's flow,

. . . . . .

An unwonted calm pervades his breast;
  And then he thinks he knows
  The hills where his life rose,
  And the sea where it goes.

The chapters which follow will interpret more fully the poise and power which come from the energizing of this centre of quiet. The Zen Buddhists have done more than most modern mystics to nurture this inward calm to attain it, and to bring life into a consistent organ by means of it. Professor Suzuki, who is a leading expert in these matters, interprets the attainment of inward calm—*Satori* as the Zen calls it—as follows:

What the Zen proposes to do is a revolution, and a revaluation as well of the spiritual aspect of one's existence. The solving of a mathematical problem ends with the solution, it does not affect one's whole life. So with all other particular questions, practical or scientific, they do not necessarily alter the basic life-tone of the individual concerned. But the opening of *Satori* is the remaking of life itself. When it is genuine—for there are many simulacra of it—its effects on one's moral and spiritual life are revolutionary, and they are also enhancing, purifying, as well as exacting.[2]

St. Paul in an exalted passage in his Corinthian correspondence says that men are meant to be co-laborers with God and to become the tilled ground—the farm, in fact—in which He brings forth here on earth "the fruits of the Spirit." There is no other place where they are produced. They do not shine in the light of the stars; they do not come down to us like Iris on the rainbow. We are no nearer the harvest of the Spirit —love, peace, joy—on the top of Mt. Everest than we are in the valley. If these supreme fruits of life are ever to emerge at all in this world they must spring out of the cultivated fields within us, where God and man meet and work together.

A remarkable instance of this "centre of repose" comes to light in the account of the transformation which came to Abraham Lincoln with the close of the Civil War. The account was written by Senator Harlan, who was the father-in-law of Robert Lincoln. He says of Lincoln:

He had suddenly become, on the fall of Richmond and the surrender of the Confederate Army, April 9, at Appomattox, a different man. His whole appearance, poise and bearing had marvelously changed. He was, in fact, transfigured. That indescribable sadness which had pre-

[2] D. T. Suzuki in an article in publications of the Eastern Buddhist Society, I, p. 196.

viously seemed to me an adamantine element of his very being had suddenly changed for an equally indescribable expression of serene joy! As if conscious that the great purpose of his life had been achieved. His countenance had become radiant, emitting spiritual light something like a halo. Yet there was no manifestation of exaltation or ecstasy. He seemed the very personification of supreme satisfaction.[3]

[3] *Mary, Wife of Lincoln,* by Katherine Helm, p. 253. By permission of Harper & Brothers.

CHAPTER X

THAT MUCH ABUSED WORD, MYSTICISM

THE confusion that attaches to the word "mysticism" is a serious handicap for one who feels compelled to use it to signify the deepest and richest stage of man's religious life, which is direct experience of God.

The earliest associations of the word are undoubtedly with the mystery religions of Greece. The person who was initiated was called a *mystes,* or *myst,* that is to say a person who now possessed the "secret." The Greek root *mu,* which in English becomes "my," means to shut or close, and in particular for matters that are revealed to the initiate it meant to close or shut the mouth, or as we should say using the same root, "keep mum," with finger on lip. When the word came to birth, then, in the sphere of early religion, it implied a person who had entered upon a hidden, secret way to an essential truth for life and salvation, but who must not make the truth public or common property. The way must remain "hidden" and the truth must be "secret," unveiled only to those on the inside.

The word, however, and its kindred forms would have lost their significance and would have dropped out of current use, if it had not been for the fact that many of the founders and fathers of the early Christian Church, living as they did in an intellectual environment in which there was a fascination, almost an infatuation, for these hidden, secret ways to peace and salvation, chose to emphasize in their writings those aspects of the Christian faith which correspond most closely to the mystery religions with which they were surrounded. They undoubtedly made use, consciously or unconsciously, of the spell of mystery which powerfully appealed to that age. St. Paul no doubt used the word "mystery" on a higher level of significance than was common in the "mystery circles" of the Ægean, but it seems obvious that he is using a well-known word, and that he is using it to take the wind out of the sails of rival societies who have their private secrets. *This is our "mystery,"* he says, *Christ in us.* St. Paul, too, plainly conceives the sacraments as mysteries, the secret of which only those who share in them can fully comprehend.

Clement of Alexandria, Gregory of Nyssa, Athanasius and Chrysostom gloried in the terms which were taken over from the mystery religions, and transferred them with new and deeper meaning to the sacraments and other services of the Church. Baptism becomes "initiation," the Communion Supper is a secret "mystery" and the Church itself is a mysterious entity which imparts grace and power to those who are sharers in its

teries had coined, and he named "contemplation" by
the well-known word "mystical" experience, which has
now become fixed in western speech.

But more significant than the selection of the word
which came to be used to designate the personal experience of God, was the process of philosophical thinking in the first four or five centuries of our era that
shaped the intellectual frame or pattern or system to
which the experience was expected to conform. The
Fathers of the Church thought of God as being absolutely perfect, and consequently as being utterly transcendent. Whether they were intellectually influenced
by Plato, or by Aristotle, or by Philo, or, at a later
period, by Plotinus and the later Neoplatonists, God
was throughout this period conceived by them as absolutely above and beyond the finite sphere. He belonged
in a purely supersensuous realm. They hoped by im-
puting to God absolute transcendency of nature to free
Him from any contact with the world of "mutability,"
and from all responsibility for the existence of *evil*.
The difficulty, however, involved in this scheme of
transcendency was that it logically made God forever
unknowable and unrevealable. Being, as they maintained, absolutely super-finite and above all the distinctions of quality and character which are known here
below, God cannot be *like* anything we know, and He
could consequently never be apprehended or expressed
in any terms familiar to a "finite" mind. No matter

how far up the mind may climb by the ladder of human intellect, God is bound to be beyond the highest rung of that ladder. He is above the topmost peak, which we can never reach. He is still "yonder" in a sphere where all finites are "transcended."

This logical situation determined for the thinkers of that time the form in which a mystical experience might be expected. Only one "way" was open, only one "approach" was conceivable. It must be by a "mysterious" way beyond the rounds of the ladder of man's mind. That rigid situation which their logic imposed involved to their minds two essential conclusions. First, that the pathway up to God must be a way of negation —a *via negativa*. We must leave behind every finite form, or symbol, or sign or image. They all fall short of the mark. In the presence of that which is the highest and best that our minds can know or think, we must say: "Nay, it will not do. God is not that." He is still "yonder," beyond all similitudes. If we ever "arrive" at the terminus it must be with empty hands, with minds purged of finitude and imagery, and by a way which lies beyond our well-known type of subject-object thought.

In the second place, as implied above, there must be an approach which transcends our usual ways of "knowing." In other words we must have a supra-rational way of passing beyond the upper end of the highest round of our mental ladder. We must leave the ladder and use "wings of flight." Plotinus used exactly that word "flight" for the last stage of the passage, "the flight of the alone to the Alone." St. Augustine called the final passage upward "a leap." "We came," he says, speaking of himself and his mother, "to our minds," by which he means the utmost reach of our minds, "and we passed beyond them with the utmost leap of our hearts." "In one trembling flash, without intermediary, we touched the Eternal Wisdom."

Plotinus consistently called this last "flight" or "leap" which takes one beyond the range of mind, "ecstasy." It is a fused, unfocussed, undifferentiated state. It is in many respects like the hypnotic state. A conscious subject aware of a specific object is no longer present. The mind is blank as to definite content and yet may be, and often is unified, concentrated, intense and filled to overbrimming with energy and rapture. St. Augustine nowhere claims to have been ecstatic himself, but he gave a good description of ecstasy, which I have taken from Dom Cuthbert Butler's great book, *Western Mysticism:*

When the attention of the mind is wholly turned away and withdrawn from the bodily senses, it is called an ecstasy. Then whatever objects may be present are not seen with the open eyes, nor any voices heard at all. It is a state midway between sleep and death: The soul is rapt in such wise as to be withdrawn from the bodily senses more than in sleep but less than in death (p. 71).

Dionysius told his disciple that he must "leave be-hind both sensible perceptions and intellectual efforts, and all objects of sense and intellect, and all things both not-being and being, and be raised aloft *unknowingly* to the union as far as attainable with Him who is above every essence and all knowledge. By resistless and abso-lute ecstasy, in all purity from thyself and everything else, thou wilt be carried above to the super-essential ray of Divine Darkness."

The dear man is obviously, as I have called him, "turgid in style," but no one can miss the plain fact that his way up is "ecstasy," or that the goal to be attained is above the reach of mind, and is a "Divine Darkness." Every finite glimmer of human light is blown out. Dionysius often calls this supra-mental state of mystical experience "Agnostia," by which he means an elevation above all knowledge, or as he says in *Mystic Theology,* "By knowing nothing, I mean *know-ing above the mind.*" We have in Dionysius the origin of the famous phrase "the cloud of unknowing," the "learned ignorance" and "the super-luminous gloom of silence," which in Eckhart becomes "the desert of the God-head where no one is at home."

This metaphysical position that God, if He is to be Perfect, must be an *absolute other—totaliter aliter—*be-yond all finite distinctions, above all known qualities, and therefore a "naked God-head," stripped of all

marks of character and forever unrevealable, brought
these noble mystics of the third, fourth and fifth centuries to this impasse which we have seen. Their system
of thought about the finite and the infinite, the here and
the yonder, determined in advance the way of approach
which mystical experience *for them* was bound to take.
Their infinite was conceived as an abstract infinite, *beyond* the finite, and stripped of all marks of distinction
or character; and in order to hope to arrive at that goal,
one must perforce go beyond mind and emerge into "a
Divine Dark." One must know in "a Cloud of Unknowing." One must climb by stripping off all finite
things and pass through, as St. John of the Cross has so
vividly indicated, "the dark night of the senses" and
"the darker night of the soul."

This *via negativa* pathway of the soul is without question the classical type of mysticism, and it has come in
the mind of many present-day interpreters to stand as
the only type of experience that can properly be called
"mysticism." In terms of this system of thought, which
completely sunders God and man, one would be bound
to define mysticism as "Belief in the possibility of
union with the Divine *by means* of ecstatic contemplation." Friedrich Heiler, who belongs in this classical
line, in his definition of mysticism, has pushed the negative aspect of it to its farthest limits. He defines mysticism as "that form of communion with God in which

the world and the self are radically negated, in which the human personality is dissolved, submerged and engulfed in the infinite one-ness of Divinity." [1]

Here, I am convinced, a metaphysical theory is voicing itself, not an experience. Mysticism has taken this form because it is dominated by a metaphysical theory. My contention always has been, and still is, that *this particular way* of approach was determined by a prevailing type of philosophical outlook, and is in no real sense essential to genuine mystical experience.

Two of my supreme intellectual guides of life, Plato and Plotinus, no doubt did much to encourage this conception of the abstract and characterless infinite, though they themselves both, in their deeper moments, held a richer view of eternal reality than that. No ancient or medieval thinker ever dealt adequately with what we have learned to call "the concrete infinite," an infinite revealed in and through the temporal and the finite. They talk as though the *perfect* must have no tinge or color of the broken lights of the imperfect. Any defining mark of character or quality seemed to imply a limitation and a drop from the sphere of perfection. The absolute reality must lie beyond all distinctions of this or that. That logically makes it *a divine Dark*.

Fortunately we have found a better way, or at least some of us have. St. John's Vine with many branches

[1] *Das Gebet*—3d Edition, p. 249.

already suggested in a figure this better way. In that
figure we have the suggestion of an Infinite that goes
out into multitudinous manifestations and that finds
itself in and through its interrelated and finite branches.
Perfection is not through isolation and withdrawal, but
through self-surrender and sacrificial limitation. If that
is a true conception we shall look for God—our God
of the Christ revelation—not above the dome of the
world, not beyond the tinge and color of life, but in
the current of it, a current that never runs smooth, in
the love and in the tragedy of this our life, immersed
as it is in the finite. If that is so, then ecstasy is not our
surest way to God, and we must profoundly reinterpret
the mystic way, though in doing it we must not forget
that these old mystics of the past, with their hampering
metaphysics, did actually in experience arrive and did
touch eternal reality.

There was, too, another factor besides the prevailing
philosophy which tended to give support to the view
that man can reach the goal of his spiritual journey only
through *ecstasy* and the way of darkness. That other
factor was the prevalence, then as now, of psychopathic
phenomena of trance, ecstasy and possession. These
mysterious phenomena are as old as the race. They
could be explained by no existing science at an earlier
time. They seemed to be produced by the finger of
God. And in all ages persons of this type have been

regarded as "prophets" and "sibyls" and "holy persons" —nearer to God than others. Complete "concentration" by means of auto-suggestion, therefore came to be regarded as a peculiarly divine gift. Ecstasy and trance were dignified, or even glorified, as a way to divine contact and the well-known experience of seeing lights and hearing voices was thought of as entrance upon a higher stage of life than the everyday level. It was easy and natural to associate such phenomena as these with the mystical way. At a time when the philosophers were giving support to the belief that God could be reached only by way of ecstasy, it might well be expected that persons who were prone to ecstasy by their unstable mental structure would swell the ranks of the mystics. Mysticism and ecstasy became synonymous terms. It is this peculiar circumstance that has in many persons' minds bracketed mysticism and abnormality under one category.

There is still one more historical trail which has left its mark on the present-day meaning of the word. Owing to its connection with the secrets of the mystery religions the word "mysticism" was very easily applied to any type of esoteric, or theosophical, "knowledge," a type of knowledge often called "gnosis." "Gnosis" is not knowledge logically or scientifically arrived at. It is not capable of open verification, nor does it possess the trait either of universality or of necessity. It is not *semper et ubique idem.* It has an aspect of caprice and of mystery. George Chapman expressed this mysterious aspect of such knowledge in his line: "Not a light shall ope the common out-way."

It is thought of by many persons as a kind of truth that "squeaks and gibbers" in hidden corners and out-of-the-way places. The fascination for this sort of thing did not disappear when the early Church conquered Gnosticism. Psychic phenomena, as I have said, are as old as the race, and persons of psychopathic structure ever since Adam's seventh son have claimed to have "revelations," "communications," "possessions," "secret knowledge" and "hidden lore." This fascination for the occult has been one of the main sources of the "infection" of the word, "mysticism."

Mystics themselves are no doubt partly to blame for the confusion. Many mystics of good standing and of lofty mystical experience have also had unstable constitutions of an abnormal type, and, consequently, have exhibited at certain stages of their life psychic phenomena of a striking order. Their disciples and biographers and, it must be said, occasionally the mystics themselves, have seized upon these occurrences as miraculous happenings and have given them an undue prominence and a place of halo. These phenomena have sometimes helped to get the "saint" canonized, though for the most part the pillar mystics themselves have discounted such psychic phenomena and have estimated them at their real worth.

Nevertheless, these things have been in the picture and they have tended to color the word with a sinister meaning. In most modern scientific laboratories the word mysticism is even now used to connote "spurious knowledge," occult lore, or abnormal phenomena. The student is given the impression that the word stands for claptrap and mental rubbish. For him it is, like an unclean leper, a thing to be forever avoided. It is obviously unfortunate to use such a "bedraggled" word for the most exalted experiences of human life. It is, however, now too late for us to coin a new English word. The habits of speech are too fixed.[2]

The best course open to us is to "disinfect" the word of its sinister meanings, or perhaps better still, to sublimate it to its higher uses. It is not the only word in our language that has been out late nights and has come back "bedraggled." "Humanism" is another outcast term which one uses at his peril. "Love" is a word that moves on many levels and yet St. Paul succeeded in sublimating it for very noble uses, though it still has a propensity to drop to a low and vulgar meaning. "Intuition" has been used to cover a very wide range of meanings, all the way from normal sense experience

[2] The German language has two words where we have but one. It uses *"Mysticismus"* for the occult and the abnormal, and *"Mystik"* for the theory of life that God and man are akin and in reciprocal relationship.

to the oracular and infallible revelation of moral duty, and so on up to the supreme height of the vision of God.

I shall now endeavor to pass the word "mysticism" through its bath of purification, and to indicate how, after a careful historical study of mystical movements, I think it ought to be used in the sphere of religion. It ought no longer to be a synonym for the "mysterious." There is still to be sure a veil of mystery over all the deepest realities in our universe, and we may well ask with the little schoolgirl, "Do I know now as much as I don't know?" But the mystery is just as deep in the realm of science as it is in the realm of religion, and we do not need another word to indicate mystery.

Nor, further, is the word needed to indicate the occult, the esoteric, or "Borderland Phenomena." "Automatic writing," or "automatic speaking," may have, and certainly often does have, a significance for psychology, but I am tired of having it forthwith treated as though it were a sure evidence of a mystical communication from God. These experiences are "psychical phenomena," but they are not in any proper sense "mystical" phenomena. Nor, again, ought the word to be limited to the specific "way" of contemplation of God and of union with Him which involves the *via negativa,* the way of abstraction and ecstasy. That specific "way" is no doubt characteristic of the classical type of mysticism. It has held an important place in the experience of the race, but ecstatic contemplation is not the *essentia* of mysticism; it is only the form imposed upon mystical experience by the prevailing philosophical and psychological framework of a given metaphysical theory. It was a well-defined mystic way, to be sure, by which saintly souls for many centuries reached a shining goal. But other souls, as saintly, have reached the same goal by a different path, a path which has as good right to be called a "mystic way," as has the "ecstatic flight."

In short, the *essentia* of mysticism ought to be thought of simply as the experience of direct communion of the soul with God. As there are great variations of degree in the definiteness of the experience, it would be safer and more modest to say that in mystical experience one finds himself in direct relationship with an Over-World of reality of the same nature as his own inmost self and with which he feels akin. Both Plato and Kant have called this "Over-World," the noumenal world, which means "the World of Mind or Spirit." The Christocentric mystics interpret this Over-World reality which breaks into their experience as "Christ," by which they mean, as St. Paul meant, the invisible eternal Christ-Spirit.

Archbishop Söderblom divided mysticism into two distinguishable types. One type, the *via negativa,* he called "mysticism of infinity," obviously abstract infinity, and the other type, "mysticism of personality." I have consistently called the former type "negation mysticism," and the latter type "affirmation mysticism." The peculiar "way" of arrival at the goal is not so important as is the actual fact of having arrived. There will always be negative aspects in any affirmation life. It is impossible to go north without "negating" the tendency to travel south. One cannot have x without the surrender of much that is not x. One cannot walk the easy path of dalliance and at the same time reap the fruits of stern concentration. There must be a stripping off of everything superfluous if you intend to venture the highest peaks, and you can arrive only after severe discipline. But I see no good reason for concluding that the God who is *found* through mystical experience is "a Divine Dark," or that He can be known only in "a cloud of unknowing."

Let me give as an illustration of affirmation mysticism the personal experience of a modern man. It very well shows the transforming power of an invading Love. It did not obliterate consciousness. It did not make life a blank. It did not culminate in ecstasy. The cup of life was filled, not emptied. The testimony is as follows: "I became conscious of a subtle change stealing over me. It was as if I were a cup which was slowly being filled with living water. I was invaded by some will in which was infinite love, peace, wisdom and power. I felt a never before known humility and gladness, an inexpressible certainty that behind and within all the discords of life, there was a divine intention and a final harmony; that the darkness in me was in this timeless moment resolved in light and the error redeemed in ultimate comprehension." [3]

One of my own students, soon after finishing college, had an experience which he has described to me as follows: "Suddenly I felt an onrush of the Universal Spirit filling me. It seemed to crush the body by its tremendous power. There was the feeling that my thoughts just previous (he had been thinking of a life as a medical missionary and a healing service) were not idle ways of the imagination, but were to be realities which would come to pass. This inflood of the Spirit went as quickly as it came and left me with a desire to be alone with thought and meditation."

Nearly all New Testament scholars now recognize that there is a profound strand of mysticism of this affirmation type in the writings of St. Paul and St. John. But it is obviously not of the classical type. It does not easily conform to the "mystical way" of the great tradition. Fifty-four times in his Letters to his Churches, St. Paul speaks of the way in which human life is *raised to a new power* when the Divine Spirit or, what for him means the same thing, when Christ, is "in us," or when we are "in Him." This experience of rising with Christ into "newness of life" is beyond

[3] Hugh Fausset—*A Modern Prelude.* Jonathan Cape, London, p. 169.

question a central feature of St. Paul's Christianity, but
it is not ecstatic, nor is it reached by a process of abstraction. Sometimes the experience comes by "invasion," as at Pentecost, when the real presence seemed
to envelope the individual soul. St. Paul describes this
experience of invasion as "Christ in you." At other
times the soul of the individual seems to break through
all barriers and come into the Spirit, or to come into
Christ, and he describes this experience of breaking
through as "being in Christ," or as "being in the Spirit."
In any case, St. Paul's Ægean Christianity moves in a
mystical sphere of life and thought, and he always implies that the Unseen and Eternal—what I have called
"the Over-World"—are more real than the temporal, and that eternity is revealed here in time through
us. "The life I now live in the flesh," St. Paul says,
"I live in the faith of the Son of God who loved me
and gave Himself for me." For St. Paul, "faith," in its
highest meaning is mystical apprehension. So far as I
can see, he never assesses the increase of power through
mystical experience in terms of rare physical phenomena, or in terms of emotional thrills or in terms of
any merely private satisfactions. The great achievement
which marks the state of "being in Christ," or of "having Christ in you," is the conquest of sin, the creation
of a new man, the attainment of "the mind of Christ,"
the acquisition of power in this difficult world to be
more than a conqueror, ability to render "reasonable

service," and, above all, to become an organ of the greatest thing in the world, love and grace.

That Ægean Christianity of St. Paul seems to me to be the very heart and essence of mystical religion. But it is affirmation, not negation. It does involve, as all spiritual process does, death to sin and to the old self, but one arrives at his goal not with consciousness blown out or personality abolished, rather with a re-created and revitalized self—changed into the same image from one stage of character to an ever higher type of character.

St. John's Gospel and his First Epistle, which Percy Gardner has called "the Ephesian Gospel," give us another interpretation of Eternity breaking into time and of human life lived in the power of the Spirit. There could hardly be a more exalted personal testimony than this man's claim to have "seen and heard and handled the Word of Life, which was from the beginning" (I John I:1), or his other testimony, "We beheld His glory the glory of the Eternal Logos, of His fulness have we received, grace upon grace" (John I:14 and 16). The believer for him is to become a living branch in an Eternal Vine. He is to be "led into all Truth" by the inward Spirit of Truth, and he is to "overcome the world," not by going away and leaving it, but by a birth from above into the Life of the Spirit who is over all. Both of these interpreters are primarily concerned for the progress of truth, for the dynamizing and construction of life, for the promotion of those inherent, intrinsic traits of character which reveal the work of the Spirit. They are not interested in ecstasy, and they do not encourage "a flight of the alone to the Alone." The closer approach to God makes a richer and completer man.

The humanistic revival with its return to the original sources gave a fresh emphasis to this milder and more affirmative type of mysticism. Erasmus, the great exponent of humanism in the North was not mystically minded, but he did much to prepare the way for a lay-religion which was deeply penetrated with direct mystical life. He was a powerful foe of corruption, ecclesiasticism, dogma and the unfree will. He accustomed his generation to an optimistic account of human nature. He made it much easier for thoughtful seekers to expect mutual and reciprocal correspondence with God. It was Hans Denck, one of his disciples, who said: "There is an inward witness which God plants in the human soul. Without this nobody would seek God, for he who seeks Him has in very truth already found Him and without this inner Guide no one even with the Bible could find Him."

This faith which Denck reveals that man possesses a spiritual endowment in his deepest inner centre runs on through Jacob Boehme, John Everard, George Fox and the greatest of the English poets, through Emerson, Whitman and William James, and is a part of our normal spiritual inheritance today. There are, it must be said, many facts of human nature which "shriek against" this optimistic creed. It is not easy after reading the morning paper to hold the faith of George Fox that "there is something of God in every man."

Nevertheless, I am firmly convinced that there is an unfathomable depth of inward Godlike being at man's spiritual centre which is the taproot of human self-consciousness and which is unsundered from this Over-World which we call God. Deeper than our faculties, more fundamental than our ideas, or our images, or our volitions, is this subsoil root of our being, this essence of the soul, this core of personality, which is indissolubly connected with a higher world of reality and is the ground of mystical experience.

This deeper stratum of our being can, like taste for art, or like appreciation of music, be cultivated, made quick and sensitive, and it can become a transmissive medium of the highest significance, or it can be buried deep under the piles of rubbish which merely secular pursuits or a life of pleasure-seeking may accumulate. If teachers and trainers of children generally held this high faith, and saw vividly the potency of the interior centre of the soul; if, knowing its importance they developed an adequate technique for cultivating its powers, we might some day have a different race of men, "no longer half-akin to brute," but capable of having a kingdom of God within them.

I am eager to have the word mysticism widened out

in meaning to include this milder and more normal correspondence of the soul with God. "We come to God," St. Augustine once said, "by love and not by navigation," and we may add, we come by ascents of faith and hope and love and not alone by flights of ecstasy. Whittier had this in mind when with a touch of real genius he wrote the lines:

> *The silence of eternity*
> *Interpreted by love.*

Evelyn Underhill has beautifully expressed the interaction of the finite and the infinite, the temporal and the eternal, in words which I should like to quote:

As we watch life, we realize how deeply this double fact of God's inciting movement and the response it invokes from us, enters into all great action; and not only that which we recognize as religious. In all heroic achievements, and all accomplishment that passes beyond the useful to seek the perfect, we are conscious of two factors which cannot be separated, but cannot be confused. There is ever a genuine and costly personal effort up to the limit of the self's endurance: and there is, inciting, supporting, and using this devoted thrust of the creature, this energetic love, a mighty invading and enveloping Power.[4]

That is exactly what I have been calling in an earlier chapter "mutual and reciprocal correspondence." It may go on within man as a silent infusion of grace

[4] *The Golden Sequence,* p. 70. By permission of E. P. Dutton, New York, and Methuen, London.

and power, or it may rise to a height of clearly conscious receptivity of incomes from beyond the margins of the self. It would no doubt have been a boon if some saint of this quiet order had invented a winged word to name this co-relationship of the soul with God, but we need not go far astray if we go on using the ancient word mysticism to express inner converse and communion with the Over-World beyond us.

LOW VISIBILITY

I HAVE recently been on a sea trip, much of the time enveloped in a thick fog. The range of visibility was extremely short. The ship crept along cautiously, feeling its way and sounding the foghorn at frequent intervals. The horn had no note of joy or triumph. It was a sound only of fear and warning. Every other ship in the neighborhood was a menace and each ship in turn was afraid of us. But while the fog lasted our ship was concerned almost wholly for its own safety. The noises it made were for its own protection, and the lower the visibility dropped the more worried everyone became for the safety of the ship to which he had committed his destiny.

The first thing that impressed me as we lived in the fog was the severe limitations which it imposed upon our life. There was no sky over us, no horizon, no color, no beauty, no proper world. If we were always doomed to live in a fog-bound world we should never know that a sun existed or a moon or the stars. There would be no astronomy. We could only guess at what caused the variations of light and darkness. We should vaguely surmise that there must be some power out beyond the veil of fog, that shifted the scenes of day and night. But no one could dream of the glory of sunrise and sunset, nor would there be any hint of the sublimity and wonder of the stars.

The slightest change in the atmosphere conditions of our world would lodge us permanently in a low visibility world like that. The raindrop which dispels the fog can form only where there is an infinitesimal particle present, around which as a tiny nucleus the moisture condenses into the rain globule, which then falls by its own weight. In perfectly pure air there could be no rain, as also there would be no color and no dome of sky. At sea it is the presence in the air of tiny fragments of salt crystals that form the nucleus for the formation of raindrops and thus serve for the clarification of the air by the deposit of moisture.

Some day, perhaps not far distant, it will almost certainly be possible by artificial means to dispel fog and to open a path of light in front of ships. Successful experiments have already been made in removing fog from small areas, but the process is expensive and the mechanism too cumbersome to be practical, but it may assuredly be predicted that the human mind will in the course of time find a way to conquer this obstacle to safety on the sea and in the air. When that time comes the ship will be able to protect itself, not by discordant and disturbing noises, but by the projection of a path of light which will give help and guidance to all near-by ships as well as safety to itself.

But this condition of low visibility at sea may very well become a parable of the spiritual climate through which we have been passing. Our visibility has plainly enough been running low. There has been a loss of sky and stars, and a very low visibility for any realities beyond the near ones. One could vaguely guess that there must be more than was revealed here within the enveloping veils of time and space, but in spite of the dim guess life has remained shut in, contracted and painfully limited both in upward reach and in stretch of horizon. Instead of trying to dissipate the mental fog and clear away the veils, we have been busy with our small concerns for self-safety and security, and with attempts to make great noises of warning and intimations of menace to all who are in the path of our onward speed.

The time has come for the projection of a path of light that will clear away the fog, open up the sky, rediscover the stars, and reveal to awakened observers that there is a celestial luminary which our self-made fogs have too long concealed from us. The greatest fog-dispelling contrivance that has ever been found for crises like this one is a new burst of moral enthusiasm, the driving energy of spiritual passion. We have been drifting about in the mists of cynicism and distrust, blowing our foghorn of despair and danger. Enthusiasm cannot, of course, be pumped up and shot out of a spigot. Moral passion is not something that can be commandeered at need. Nor shall we pass from dense fog to open sky by a lift of our own bootstraps, or, to change the figure, by a puff of our own breath on our sails.

I obviously omitted an important factor when I spoke of projects for dispelling fog by human effort. They may work eventually within a very limited area. In any case they show man's unconquerable spirit. But, after all, "the important factor" is the cosmic drive against the fog, which effects what man with all his powers could never do. The sun fights it from above. The shifts of temperature doom it. The currents of air and sea settle its fate. The tiny crystals of salt from the spray carry it away in little globules of rain. A few moments ago we were immersed in it and now the blue sky is over us. The horizon is a perfect circle, the air is as clear and bright as the stones in the walls of the New Jerusalem. The cosmic drive has accomplished what no enginery of man could have done.

It is so, too, with this other fog which besets us and envelopes us round. Our own efforts are all to the good. Our moral enthusiasms are noble, our spiritual passions count for something. But the best of it all is, there is cosmic free grace working for us. A realm of a higher order is over and around us. The celestial luminary of that realm, Who is the source and fountain of love, is forever breaking through the veils and working for us even when we fail to see His light and love. Our best line of action and coöperation is to become quick and acute to note His revelations. What we need most just now is to discover or rediscover where He has broken in and manifested the grace by which we can conquer and dispel the darkness.